CAMBRIDGE
UNIVERSITY PRESS

Biology

for Cambridge International AS & A Level

PRACTICAL WORKBOOK

Mary Jones & Matthew Parkin

CAMBRIDGE
UNIVERSITY PRESS

University Printing House, Cambridge CB2 8BS, United Kingdom

One Liberty Plaza, 20th Floor, New York, NY 10006, USA

477 Williamstown Road, Port Melbourne, VIC 3207, Australia

314–321, 3rd Floor, Plot 3, Splendor Forum, Jasola District Centre,
New Delhi – 110025, India

103 Penang Road, #05-06/07, Visioncrest Commercial, Singapore 238467

Cambridge University Press is part of the University of Cambridge.

It furthers the University's mission by disseminating knowledge in the pursuit of
education,learning and research at the highest international levels of excellence.

www.cambridge.org
Information on this title: www.cambridge.org/9781108797771

First published 2020

20 19 18 17 16 15 14 13 12 11 10 9 8 7 6 5 4

Printed in Italy by Rotolito S.p.A.

A catalogue record for this publication is available from the British Library

ISBN 978-1-108-79777-1 Practical Workbook Paperback

Additional resources for this publication at www.cambridge.org/9781108797771

Cambridge University Press has no responsibility for the persistence or accuracy
of URLs for external or third-party internet websites referred to in this publication,
and does not guarantee that any content on such websites is, or will remain,
accurate or appropriate. Information regarding prices, travel timetables, and other
factual information given in this work is correct at the time of first printing but
Cambridge University Press does not guarantee the accuracy of such information
thereafter.

....

DEDICATED TEACHER AWARDS

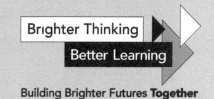

⟩ Contents

11 Inheritance, selection and evolution

12 Ecology

> How to use this series

This suite of resources supports students and teachers following the Cambridge International AS & A Level Biology syllabus (9700). All of the books in the series work together to help students develop the necessary knowledge and scientific skills required for this subject. With clear language and style, they are designed for international learners.

The coursebook provides comprehensive support for the full Cambridge International AS & A Level Biology syllabus (9700). It clearly explains facts, concepts and practical techniques, and uses real-world examples of scientific principles. Two chapters provide full guidance to help students develop investigative skills. Questions within each chapter help them to develop their understanding, while exam-style questions provide essential practice.

The workbook contains over 100 exercises and exam-style questions, carefully constructed to help learners develop the skills that they need as they progress through their Biology course. The exercises also help students develop understanding of the meaning of various command words used in questions, and provide practice in responding appropriately to these.

This write-in book provides students with a wealth of hands-on practical work, giving them full guidance and support that will help them to develop all of the essential investigative skills. These skills include planning investigations, selecting and handling apparatus, creating hypotheses, recording and displaying results, and analysing and evaluating data.

The teacher's resource supports and enhances the questions and practical activities in the coursebook. This resource includes detailed lesson ideas, as well as answers and exemplar data for all questions and activities in the coursebook and workbook. The practical teacher's guide, included with this resource, provides support for the practical activities and experiments in the practical workbook.

Teaching notes for each topic area include a suggested teaching plan, ideas for active learning and formative assessment, links to resources, ideas for lesson starters and plenaries, differentiation, lists of common misconceptions and suggestions for homework activities. Answers are included for every question and exercise in the coursebook, workbook and practical workbook. Detailed support is provided for preparing and carrying out for all the investigations in the practical workbook, including tips for getting things to work well, and a set of sample results that can be used if students cannot do the experiment, or fail to collect results.

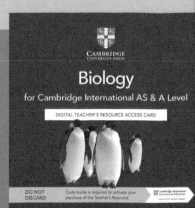

> How to use this book

Throughout this book, you will notice lots of different features that will help advance your practical skills. These are explained below.

CHAPTER OUTLINE

These appear at the start of every chapter to help you navigate the content and how the investigations relate to the Coursebook chapters.

TIPS

The information in these boxes will help you complete the investigations and give you support in areas that you might find difficult.

KEY WORDS

Key vocabulary is highlighted in the text when it is first introduced. Definitions are then given in the margin, which explain the meanings of these words and phrases

You will also find definitions of these words in the Glossary at the back of this book

Investigations

Appearing throughout this book, these help you develop practical skills which are essential for studying Cambridge AS & A Level Biology.

The investigations contain an introduction which outlines the theory behind the practical work, a list of equipment, important safety advice to ensure you stay safe whilst conducting practical work, a step-by-step method, space to record your results, and finally Data analysis and Evaluation questions which help you to interpret your results. The later chapters also contain Planning investigations, which allow you to practise planning your own practical work.

> Introduction

The science of biology is often defined as the study of the structure and behaviour of the natural world through observation and experimentation. Practical work is a very important part of any biology course. Carrying out practical work helps to give you a better understanding of how scientists think and a better understanding of the theory in your course.

This book has several aims:

- to guide you through all the specific experiments that are listed in the Cambridge International AS & A Level Biology syllabus for examination from 2022. These are experiments that you need to know both for your written and practical exams.

- to help you develop an understanding of all the practical techniques that you are expected to know, such as how to perform serial dilutions, calculate magnifications and draw cells and tissues.

- to help you learn how to plan valid, safe, reliable experiments, record your results and analyse your data correctly.

- to help you to understand the topic areas better by carrying out your own observations.

Practical work in biology can often be a little different to practical work in the other sciences. Living things, by definition, show great variation, and sometimes experiments may not yield exactly the results you expect. Always remember that science is about observation and a search for truth. Even although results may not be what you expected, you should try to explain them according to what they suggest and not what you think they should have been. If results are unexpected, it is perfectly acceptable to comment on why you think this may be and try to think of ways to extend or alter your experiment to improve it.

There may be some experiments listed in the book that you are not able to perform due to not having a piece of equipment. To help with this, your teacher will have sets of results for you to analyse, and there are many demonstrations of particular techniques that you can watch on the Internet.

Working through all the experiments in this book is an excellent opportunity to develop your practical skills, and to recognise that studying biology can be fun and fulfilling in its own right. Living things surround us, and we are also part of biology. Try to enjoy each experiment and use them as a launch pad for your own research, investigations, creativity and further experiments.

> Safety

Laboratories are generally one of the places in the school where accidents are least likely to happen. (The most dangerous place, as far as the frequency of accidents is concerned, is outside the buildings.) This is because teachers and learners follow sets of rules in laboratories that are designed to keep everyone safe. It is essential that you always, without exception, follow all of the rules set out and displayed in the laboratories where you are working.

Making an assessment of the degree of risk associated with biology investigations is one of the skills that is assessed in Paper 3 and Paper 5. You should learn to think about risk every time you carry out an investigation. Once any risks have been identified, you then need to consider how you will reduce the level of risk. Most biology investigations are low risk, but some may involve a medium level of risk.

General rules for good practice

- You should *always* wear safety glasses when using liquids of any kind.

- If you have long hair, keep it tied back.

- You may also like to wear a protective laboratory coat, so that any spills do not get onto your clothes.

- Make sure that you understand any specific risks associated with the experiment, as explained by your teacher (see Table S1).

Table S1 lists some of the common sources of risk associated with biology investigations.

Source of risk	How to reduce risk	Comments
Glassware and sharp blades	Keep glassware on a laboratory surface – do not carry it around unnecessarily. Treat sharp blades, for example scalpel blades, knives or razor blades, with care. Place the object you are cutting on a surface, such a chopping board or tile, when you are cutting it – do not hold it in your hand. Always cut away from you, so that if the blade slips it does not hit your skin. Avoid allowing reagents or liquids derived from specimens to come into contact with cuts or grazes on your skin.	Pushing glass tubing into a tight hole in a rubber bung is risky – it is best if the laboratory technician or your teacher does this, rather than doing it yourself.

Source of risk	How to reduce risk	Comments
Hot liquids (e.g. hot water in a water bath)	Keep hot liquids safely on a bench – do not carry them around. Use tongs when moving tubes into or out of very hot water baths. Do not sit down when carrying out practical work, unless you are doing a drawing, for example, as you can move faster to avoid spills if you are standing up.	
Chemicals	Keep all chemicals you are using in their labelled bottles. If you transfer a potentially hazardous chemical to another container, label the container first. When you remove the top from a container, place it upside down on the bench, so that its lower surface does not transfer any chemical to the bench surface.	Your teacher will know the precise level and type of risk posed by each chemical that you are using. Follow all safety instructions provided by your teacher.
Working with living organisms or material derived from them	Be aware of any allergies that you may have (e.g. to nuts, eggs or enzymes), and make sure that your teacher also knows about them. If collecting plants or animals from their habitats, make sure that you are able to recognise anything that might be poisonous, or that can sting or bite.	You may like to wear nitrile or latex gloves when working with biological specimens or substances derived from them. Boots or long socks are a good idea when working outdoors, particularly in long vegetation. If using living organisms in practical work, always treat them ethically and with respect.
Working outdoors	Always work with a partner when outside. If one of you gets into difficulties, the other can call or search for help.	

Table S1: Common sources of risk in biology investigations.

> Practical skills

Planning

- Always identify the independent and dependent variables.
- State the range and interval for your independent variable, and describe how you will achieve this.
- If possible, use at least five different values for the independent variable, with equal intervals.
- List the genuinely important variables that you should standardise and how you will do this.

Recording data

- Use a pencil and ruler to draw a results chart.
- Independent variable goes into the first column (or row), followed by dependent variable.
- Headings include units; no units in the body of the table.
- Record all values to the appropriate number of significant figures or decimal places.

Recording observations

- If recording qualitative results in a table, use short, clear descriptions.
- Draw using a medium–hard (HB) pencil, with a good quality eraser to hand.
- Draw what you can see, not what you think you ought to see.
- All lines on a drawing must be clean and clear, with no breaks or overlaps.
- Never use shading on a drawing.
- Take time to get proportions of different structures or areas correct on your drawings; for example, you can use an eyepiece graticule to make measurements of the relative widths of different tissues.
- Draw label lines with a ruler; no arrowheads; ensure the line touches the structure it is labelling.
- Use most of the space allocated for your drawing, with enough space around it for labels; labels should not be written on top of the drawing.
- Low-power plans show tissue outlines only, with no individual cells. High-power drawings show internal detail of individual cells, where visible.

Calculations

- Show every step in your calculation clearly.

- Calculated values (including means) must have the same number of significant figures as raw results, or one more.

- Do not include anomalous results in calculations; identify the result and state that you have not included it and why. You can identify anomalous data using standard deviation (mean ± 2SD to create a range of values - any raw data outside this is anomalous.)

Graphs and charts

- Construct all graphs and charts in pencil.

- Use a line graph where the variables on both axes are continuous.

- Use a bar chart where the x-axis variable is discontinuous. Bars do not touch and should not be shaded.

- Independent variable goes on the x-axis and dependent variable on the y-axis.

- Scales should be chosen to make as much use of the width and height of the grid provided as possible.

- Scales should go up in equal intervals. Intervals should be chosen so that it is easy to read intermediate points, for example going up in 2, 10, 50s and so on.

- Label both axes fully (you can often copy the headings from the results chart) and include units.

- Plot points on a line graph as small, neat crosses that intersect exactly on the required point. (Alternatively, use a dot with a circle around it.)

- Check if there are instructions telling you whether to draw a best-fit line or a set of ruled straight lines joining points.

- In general, we only draw a best-fit line when the points clearly follow a definite pattern. If you are unsure of this, then join points with ruled straight lines between the points.

- Do not extrapolate (extend the line beyond your data points) unless you are told to do so, or unless you are absolutely certain that it is reasonable to do so.

Key practical skills

Table P1 shows where each skill is most fully explained. This is usually the first time that the skill is addressed. The skill is then revisited several times in practical investigations later in the book.

Practical skill	Where to find detailed descriptions and explanations
Using a microscope	Practical Investigation 1.1
Using and calibrating an eyepiece graticule	Practical Investigation 1.1
Calculating magnification	Practical Investigation 1.1
Making serial dilutions	Practical Investigations 2.2 and 2.3
Plotting a line graph	Practical Investigation 3.1
Identifying random and systematic errors	Practical Investigation 3.1
Calculating percentage change	Practical Investigation 4.1
Drawing low power plan diagrams	Practical Investigation 6.1
Using an eyepiece graticule to estimate proportions	Practical Investigation 6.1
Drawing high-power diagrams	Practical Investigation 6.2

Table P1: Key practical skills.

Microscopy

Practical Investigation 1.1: Making a temporary slide and drawing cells

In this activity, you will practise using a light microscope. You will also make a temporary mount of plant tissue, observe it using the microscope and make a drawing of some of the cells.

YOU WILL NEED

Equipment:
• a light microscope • a source of light (this could be built into the microscope, or a lamp, or bright light from a window) • two or three microscope slides • two or three coverslips • a dropper pipette • a mounted needle or seeker • forceps (tweezers) • sharp scissors or a blade (safety razor or scalpel) • filter paper or paper towel • tile • some pieces cut from an onion bulb • a medium–hard (HB) pencil • a good quality eraser

Safety considerations

- Make sure you have read the Safety advice section at the beginning of this book and listen to any advice from your teacher before carrying out this investigation.

- Take care when using a sharp blade to cut the onion epidermis.

Method

Part 1: Making a temporary slide and viewing it through a microscope

Figure 1.1 shows the parts of a microscope.

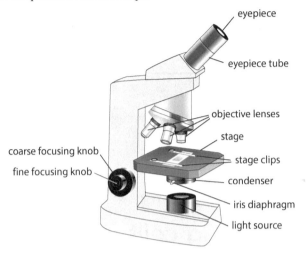

Figure 1.1: A light microscope.

1 Set up your microscope on the bench. Look for each of the parts that are labelled on the diagram.

2 You are now going to make a slide that you can view through your microscope.

   • Take a piece of one of the layers from inside an onion bulb. Using scissors or a sharp blade, cut out one piece measuring approximately 1 cm × 1 cm.

   • Using a dropper pipette, place a drop of water onto the centre of a clean microscope slide.

   • Using forceps, gently peel away the very thin layer of epidermis on the inside surface of the piece of onion. *Immediately* place the epidermis into the drop of water on the slide. Use a mounted needle or seeker to gently spread out the epidermis, so that it is not folded over and is covered by water. You may need to add another drop of water to it.

   • Gently lower a coverslip onto the slide, to cover the onion epidermis. It's a good idea to use a mounted needle (see Figure 1.2) as this helps to avoid trapping any air bubbles. If any air bubbles do occur, you should ignore these when making drawings – they will resemble car tyres under the microscope.

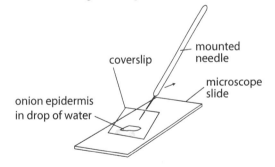

Figure 1.2: Lowering a coverslip.

> **TIP**
>
> Your microscope will almost certainly not be the same as the one in Figure 1.1. For example, it may have a mirror instead of a light source.

- Use filter paper to gently remove any water from the top of the coverslip or on the surface of the slide.

3 Now you can look at your slide through the microscope.

- Turn the objective lenses so that the smallest one is over the hole in the stage.

- Look down through the eyepiece and make sure that you can see light. If you cannot see light, adjust the light source or the mirror.

- Place your slide on the microscope stage, with the epidermis over the hole.

- Looking from the side of the microscope, turn the coarse focusing knob to lower the objective lens, until the objective lens is almost touching the slide.

- Look down the eyepiece again. Slowly turn the coarse focusing knob the other way, to raise the objective lens. Stop when you can see the epidermis. It will probably not look clear.

- Now turn the fine focusing knob until you can see the epidermis clearly. You should be able to see something similar to Figure 1.3.

TIP

If you leave water on the surface of the slide, this may get onto the objective lens. Over time, deposits may form on the lens.

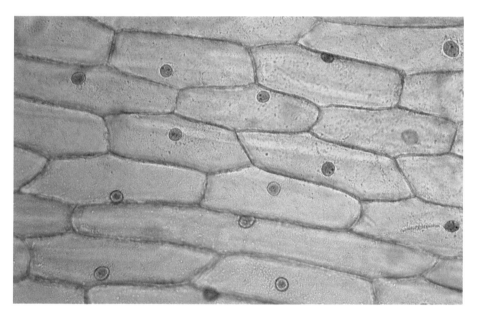

Figure 1.3: Micrograph of epidermal cells.

TIP

With some microscopes, it is possible to lower the objective lens so much that you can crash into the slide and break the coverslip. If you look from the side, it is less likely you will do this.

Part 2: Making a high-power drawing of onion epidermis

1 Focus on the onion epidermis using the lowest power objective, as described previously. Carefully swing the objective lenses around until the next largest one is over the slide. Focus using the fine focusing knob.

2 Decide which objective provides the best view of the epidermis. If you have an even higher power objective lens, you could try that one as well.

3 Make a drawing of the epidermis in the space that follows.

- Use a medium–hard (HB), sharp pencil.

- Use a high-quality eraser, so that you can completely remove any mistakes in your drawing.

TIP

It is sometimes a good idea to keep changing the objective lens as you do your drawing. For example, you may decide to use the lowest power lens, but occasionally change up to the higher power lenses to check on the detail.

- Your drawing should be large, using at least 50% of the space available – but make sure you leave enough space around it for your labels.

- Take care to get the shapes and proportions of the cells correct.

- All lines should be single and clear. Do not leave any gaps, however small, in the lines.

- Always show the cell walls with two lines – cell walls have thickness.

- Do not shade anything at all in your drawing.

- Draw what you can see, not what you think you should see.

4   Label the cytoplasm, nucleus and cell wall on your drawing.

- Use a pencil for the label lines. You may also like to use a pencil to write the names.

- Use a ruler to draw the label lines. Make sure that the end of the label line touches the part that you are labelling.

- Keep label lines separate from each other.

- The label lines can go in any direction, but the written labels should be horizontal.

Part 3: Adding a stain to a temporary slide

You are going to add some iodine in potassium iodide solution to your onion epidermis slide. This will stain (colour) any starch grains in the onion cells blue–black.

1   Place a small drop of iodine solution on the microscope slide, touching the edge of the coverslip.

2   Very carefully place one edge of a piece of a filter paper against the *opposite* side of the coverslip, as shown in Figure 1.4. The water underneath the coverslip will soak into the filter paper, bringing through the iodine solution.

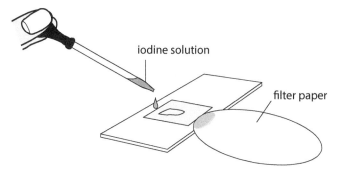

iodine solution

filter paper

Figure 1.4: Adding iodine solution.

3   Clean the slide, and then observe the stained onion epidermis through the microscope. Describe any differences you can see in the stained cells compared with their appearance before staining.

....

....

....

....

Practical Investigation 1.2: Measuring cells, using an eyepiece graticule and stage micrometer

In this activity, you will use an **eyepiece graticule** and **stage micrometer** to measure two types of plant cell. An eyepiece graticule is a little scale that fits inside the eyepiece of your microscope. When you look through the eyepiece, you can see the scale on the graticule at the same time as the object on the microscope stage. You can measure the size of the object in 'eyepiece graticule units'.

You then need to **calibrate** these graticule units. You do this using a stage micrometer. This is a slide with a scale with very small divisions on it, which you place on the microscope stage. The markings on this scale are very precisely drawn, and we know exactly how far apart they are.

KEY WORDS

eyepiece graticule: small scale that is placed in a microscope eyepiece

stage micrometer: very small, accurately drawn scale of known dimensions, engraved on a microscope slide

calibrate: convert the readings on a scale to a standard scale with known units

> **YOU WILL NEED**
>
> **Equipment:**
> • microscope, with a graticule in the eyepiece • prepared slide of section through a leaf • onion epidermis slide from Practical Investigation 1.1
>
> **Access to:**
> • a stage micrometer

Safety considerations

- Make sure you have read the Safety advice section at the beginning of this book and listen to any advice from your teacher before carrying out this investigation.

- There are no significant safety issues for this practical investigation.

Method

Part 1 : Measuring cells using an eyepiece graticule

1   Place a prepared slide of a transverse section through a leaf onto the stage of your microscope.

2   Check that there is an eyepiece graticule inside the eyepiece of your microscope. Look down through the eyepiece and turn it around. You should see the scale on the eyepiece graticule turning around.

3   Using the smallest objective lens, focus on the leaf section. Move the slide until you can see palisade cells. If necessary, change to a different objective lens, until you can see a group of palisade cells clearly. Move the slide until the cells are placed vertically.

4   Turn the eyepiece graticule until the scale lies horizontally across the group of cells, as shown in Figure 1.5.

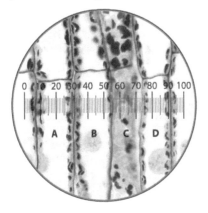

Figure 1.5: Micrograph of palisade cells seen using an eyepiece graticule.

5   Move the slide until the 0 on the graticule scale lies exactly over the cell wall of one cell. Use the scale to measure the width of three or four cells in eyepiece graticule units.

.... palisade cells measure .... graticule units.

Part 2: Calibrating the eyepiece graticule

1 Keeping the same objective lens over the slide, remove the slide from the stage and replace it with a stage micrometer.

2 Look down the eyepiece and focus on the stage micrometer scale. Move the eyepiece and/or the slide until the eyepiece graticule scale and the stage micrometer scale lie exactly next to each other, as shown in Figure 1.6.

TIP

If you get confused about which scale is the eyepiece graticule, and which is the stage micrometer, just turn the eyepiece. The scale that goes round is the eyepiece graticule scale.

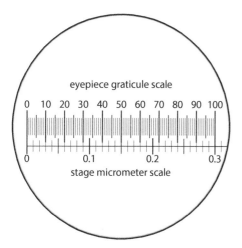

Figure 1.6: Stage micrometer seen using an eyepiece graticule.

3 Look for a good alignment of marks on the two scales, as far apart as possible. In the example in Figure 1.6, there is alignment at 0, 0 and at 80 on the eyepiece graticule scale and 0.24 on the stage micrometer scale.

Write down the alignments on your scales:

4 The large divisions on the stage micrometer scale are 0.1 mm apart. The small divisions are 0.01 mm apart.

$$0.01\,mm = 0.01 \times 10^3\,m = 10\,\mu m$$

Use this information to calculate how many μm are represented by one small division on the eyepiece graticule scale.

1 small eyepiece graticule unit = ... μm

5   Go back to the measurement you made at the end of Part 1, where you measured the width of three or four cells in eyepiece graticule units.

Convert this measurement to μm.

.... palisade cells measure .... μm.

6   Divide this value by the number of cells, to find the mean width of one palisade cell.

Mean width of one palisade cell = ... μm

7   Remove the stage micrometer from the microscope. Place a slide of onion epidermis cells onto the stage. *Using the same objective lens* as you did for the palisade cells, measure the width of a group of cells in graticule units.

.... onion epidermis cells measure .... eyepiece graticule units.

8   Convert this measurement to μm, and then calculate the mean width of one onion epidermis cell.

Mean width of one onion epidermis cell = ... μm

Part 3: Calculating the magnification of a drawing

The **magnification** of an image is the number of times larger it is than the actual object.

magnification = size of image ÷ size of actual object

1   Measure the width of the group of onion cells in your drawing in Practical Investigation 1.1. Record your answer in mm, and then multiply by 10^3 to convert it to μm.

Width of .... cells in the drawing is .... mm = ... μm.

2   Use your answer in Step 8 in Part 2 of this practical investigation to calculate the magnification of your drawing.

KEY WORD
magnification: the number of times larger an image of an object is than the real size of the object

....

Practical Investigation 1.3: Comparing animal cells and plant cells

In this activity, you will prepare a temporary slide of human cheek cells, and compare their size and structure with palisade cells and onion epidermis cells.

YOU WILL NEED

Equipment:

• microscope, with a graticule in the eyepiece • prepared slide of section through a leaf • onion epidermis slide from Practical Investigation 1.1 (or you can make a new one) • clean microscope slides and coverslips • dropper pipette • iodine in potassium iodide solution • methylene blue stain • cotton bud or similar

Access to:

• a stage micrometer

Safety considerations

- Make sure you have read the Safety advice section at the beginning of this book and listen to any advice from your teacher before carrying out this investigation.

- There is a very small risk of pathogenic organisms in the saliva and cheek cell sample on the cotton bud. Place the bud in a container of disinfectant immediately after use.

Method

Part 1: Observing, recording and measuring cheek cells

1   Gently rub a cotton bud around the inside of your cheeks, as shown in Figure 1.7.

2   Rub the cotton bud onto the centre of a clean microscope slide. Note: you will not be able to see very much on the slide, but there should be a few cheek cells present. Place the bud in a container of disinfectant immediately after use.

3   Add a small drop or two of methylene blue stain to the part of the slide where you rubbed the cotton bud. This stain is absorbed by living cells. More is taken up by the nucleus than by the cytoplasm, so it makes the nucleus look dark blue and the cytoplasm pale blue.

4   Carefully lower the coverslip onto the slide (see Figure 1.2), trying to avoid trapping air bubbles. Clean the slide and coverslip using filter paper.

Figure 1.7: Method for taking a sample of cheek cells.

5   Look at the slide through the microscope. These cells are much smaller than the plant cells you have looked at earlier, so you may need to use a larger objective lens to view them.

In the space below, make a large labelled drawing of three or four cheek cells.

6   Use the eyepiece graticule to measure the diameter of three cheek cells in graticule units. (The cells will not be arranged in a neat row as in Practical Investigation 1.2, so you will have to measure each one separately.) Calculate the mean diameter of one cheek cell, in eyepiece graticule units.

....

7 Now use the stage micrometer scale to convert the eyepiece graticule units to μm. (If you used the same objective lens as for the calculation in Practical Investigation 1.2, you can use the same conversion factor. However, if you have used a different objective lens when measuring the cheek cells, you will need to follow Steps 1–4 in Practical Investigation 1.2, Part 2 for this objective lens.)

....

8 Use your answers to Steps 6 and 7 to calculate the mean diameter of a cheek cell in μm.

....

9 Calculate the magnification of your drawing from Step 5. Show your working.

....

Part 2: Comparing cheek cells, palisade cells and onion epidermis cells

You are going to construct a table to compare the size and visible structures in the three types of cell you have been observing and measuring.

1   Using a ruler and pencil, draw a table with four columns in the space that follows. Label the first column 'Feature', and the other three columns with the type of cell.

2   On a piece of rough paper, make a note of possible features that you can compare. These could include the sizes of the cells, their shapes, the relative size of the nucleus compared with the size of the entire cell, the structures visible inside the cells, and the way the cells are grouped together. Remember that a comparison includes similarities as well as differences.

3   Complete your table to compare the three types of cell. Draw a ruled line beneath each set of features, so that it is easy for someone else to understand the information you are listing.

> **TIP**
>
> If you have time, you could try staining cheek cells with iodine solution, or onion epidermis cells with methylene blue stain.

Chapter 2
Biological molecules

This chapter relates to Chapter 2: Biological molecules, in the Coursebook.
In this chapter, you will complete practical investigations on:

- 2.1 The biochemical tests used to identify different biological molecules

- 2.2 The semi-quantitative Benedict's test and serial dilutions

- 2.3 Using a semi-quantitative **iodine test** to compare the starch content of bananas.

Practical Investigation 2.1: The biochemical tests used to identify different biological molecules

It is important to be able to identify common biological molecules. You need to know the biochemical tests for starch, reducing sugars, non-reducing sugars, proteins and fats. All these are **qualitative tests** and only give an idea of the presence or absence of a molecule rather than the quantity.

KEY WORDS

iodine test: a test for starch. Iodine solution turns a blue-black colour in the presence of starch

qualitative test: a test that gives a non-numerical description of something (e.g. the intensity of a colour)

YOU WILL NEED

Equipment:
- Ten test tubes • test-tube rack • Bunsen burner, tripod, gauze, heat-proof tile • test-tube holder • glass beakers, 500 and 50 cm^3 • pipette, 10 cm^3, and pipette filler • Benedict's solution, 25 cm^3 • biuret solution, 25 cm^3 • iodine solution in a dropper bottle • ethanol, 200 cm^3 • distilled water, 50 cm^3 • dilute hydrochloric acid in a dropper bottle • sodium hydrogencarbonate (solid) • spatula • 20 cm^3 of 1% starch solution, 1% protein solution (albumin or casein), vegetable oil, 10% glucose, 10% fructose, 10% sucrose, 10% lactose, 10% maltose • 'unknown' solutions X, Y and Z, 20 cm^3

Access to:
- tap water, sink (to throw away solutions)

Safety considerations

- Make sure you have read the Safety advice section at the beginning of this book and listen to any advice from your teacher before carrying out this investigation.

- If you splash solution on skin, wash it off with water. Tie back long hair, and use Bunsen burners with care.

- Iodine solution should not be thrown away in water that could come into contact with aquatic life.

- Biuret solution is an irritant and should be handled carefully.

- Sodium hydroxide is corrosive and it is essential that eye protection is worn. If you splash sodium hydroxide into your eyes, wash eyes with lots of running water.

- Ethanol is highly flammable and so only carry out the lipid test when there are no naked flames (e.g. Bunsen burners).

Method

Part 1: The iodine test for starch

1   Label three test tubes 1–3.

2   Using a pipette, place $5\,cm^3$ of 1% starch suspension into the test tube labelled '1'.

3   Wash the pipette with water.

4   Place $5\,cm^3$ 10% glucose solution into test tube 2, again washing the pipette.

5   Place $5\,cm^3$ distilled water into test tube 3.

6   Place five drops of iodine solution into each tube. Mix each tube.

7   Record the colours of each tube in Table 2.1 of the Results section.

Part 2: The biuret test for proteins

The **biuret test** for proteins can be carried out by adding a mixture of copper sulphate and sodium hydroxide (as biuret solution) or by adding the two solutions separately.

1   Label three test tubes 1–3.

2   Using a pipette, place $5\,cm^3$ of 1% protein solution into tube 1.

3   Wash the pipette with water.

4   Place $5\,cm^3$ 10% glucose solution into tube 2, again washing the pipette.

5   Place $5\,cm^3$ distilled water into test tube 3.

6   Place $5\,cm^3$ biuret solution[2] into each tube and mix.

7   Record the colours of each solution in Table 2.1.

Part 3: The reducing sugar test

Some sugars can donate electrons to other chemicals; this means that the sugars are reducing agents. In **Benedict's solution**, soluble Cu^{2+} ions are blue. If these Cu^{2+} ions gain an electron, they become Cu^+ ions which are red and insoluble.

1   Label six test tubes 1–6.

2   Using a pipette, place $5\,cm^3$ of 10% glucose solution into tube 1. Wash the pipette with water.

3   Place $5\,cm^3$ sucrose, maltose, fructose, lactose and water into tubes 2–5, washing the pipette each time.

4   Place $5\,cm^3$ distilled water into test tube 6.

5   Add $5\,cm^3$ Benedict's solution to each tube.

6   Set up a boiling water bath by filling the $500\,cm^3$ beaker half full of water. Heat it using the Bunsen burner, tripod, gauze and heatproof mat as shown in Figure 2.1.

KEY WORDS

iodine test: a test for starch. Iodine solution turns a blue-black colour in the presence of starch

biuret test: a test for the presence of amine groups and thus for the presence of proteins; biuret reagent is added to the unknown substance, and a change from pale blue to purple indicates the presence of proteins

Benedict's solution: a test for the presence of reducing sugars; the unknown substance is heated with Benedict's reagent, and a change from a clear blue solution to the production of a yellow, red or brown precipitate indicates the presence of reducing sugars such as glucose

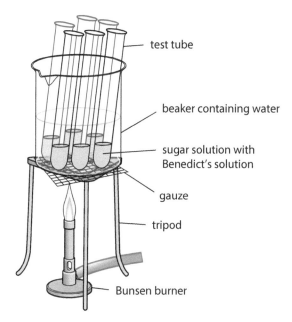

test tube

beaker containing water

sugar solution with
Benedict's solution

gauze

tripod

Bunsen burner

Figure 2.1: Apparatus for Part 3 of investigation 2.1.

TIP

It is very dangerous
to heat the test tubes
with just a bunsen
burner, so you must
use a water bath here.

7   When the water bath is boiling, carefully place the test tubes into it.

8   After 5 min, turn off the Bunsen burner and carefully remove the test tubes using a test-tube holder. Place the test tubes into a rack.

9   Record the colour and consistency (cloudy or clear) of each solution in Table 2.1.

Part 4: The non-reducing sugar test

1   Label two test tubes 1 and 2.

2   Using a pipette, place $5\,cm^3$ distilled water into tube 1 and $5\,cm^3$ 10% sucrose solution into test tube 2.

3   Place two drops of dilute hydrochloric acid into each tube.

4   Set up a boiling water bath.

5   Carefully place the tubes into the boiling water bath for 2 min.

6   Remove the tubes and place them into a rack.

7   Using a spatula, tap small amounts of solid sodium hydrogencarbonate into the solutions until they no longer fizz (this neutralises the acid).

8   Using a pipette, add $5\,cm^3$ Benedict's solution to each tube.

9   Place the tubes into the boiling water bath for 5 min.

10 Turn off the Bunsen burner and carefully remove the test tubes.

11 Record the colour and consistency of each solution in Table 2.1.

TIP

Remember that if
you are testing for
non-reducing sugars,
you need to do a
Benedict's test first to
show that there are
no reducing sugars
present.

Part 5: The emulsion test for lipids (fats and oils)

1   Label two test tubes 1 and 2.

2   Using a pipette, place $5\,cm^3$ ethanol into each tube.

3   Add two drops of vegetable oil to tube 1 and mix thoroughly to dissolve the oil in the alcohol.

4   Add $5\,cm^3$ water to each tube and mix thoroughly.

5   Record the colour and consistency of each solution in Table 2.1.

Part 6: Testing the 'unknown' solutions

1   There are three solutions labelled X, Y and Z.

2   The solutions contain different combinations of starch, protein, sucrose and glucose.

3   Carry out biochemical tests to determine the contents of each solution.

4   Draw a results table for these three solutions in the space after Table 2.1.

Results

Biological molecule	Final colour of solution after biochemical test				
	iodine	biuret	reducing sugar	non-reducing sugar	emulsion test
1% starch					
1% protein					
10% glucose					
10% fructose					
10% maltose					
10% lactose					
10% sucrose					
vegetable oil					
water					
ethanol					

Table 2.1: Results table.

Draw up a results table for your 'unknown' solutions in the following space. Give your table headings. The first column should be given the heading 'Solution'.

Analysis, conclusion and evaluation

a   i   Look at your table of results and use it to decide what substances were in each unknown solution.

Contents of unknown solution X ....

Contents of unknown solution Y ....

Contents of unknown solution Z ....

   ii   Why can you not be certain as to the presence or absence of sucrose in solutions X and Z?

....

....

b   Use your completed Table 2.1 to complete the following:

   •   Monosaccharides that are reducing sugars include:

....

   •   Disaccharides that are reducing sugars include:

....

   •   Disaccharides that are non-reducing sugars include:

....

> **TIP**
>
> The reducing sugar test works because Benedict's solution contains dissolved Cu^{2+} ions which are blue in colour. Some sugar molecules are able to donate electrons to the Cu^{2+} ions making them red, insoluble Cu^+ ions. This means that a red precipitate forms.

c   Explain why each biochemical test (except the emulsion test) was also carried out with water.

....

....

d   Explain whether these biochemical tests are qualitative or quantitative.

....

e   The non-reducing sugar test should have given a positive result with both glucose and sucrose.

   i   Explain why glucose produced a positive result.

   ....

   ii   Explain why sucrose produces a positive result in the non-reducing sugar test but a negative result in the reducing sugar test.

   ....

   ....

   iii Describe how you could use the biochemical tests to distinguish between a solution of glucose and a solution of sucrose.

   ....

   ....

f   A student carried out a reducing sugar test on a sample of an unknown solution. This produced a positive result. They then carried out a non-reducing sugar test on another sample of the same solution. This produced a positive result but with a lot more precipitate. Explain this result.

   ....

   ....

Practical Investigation 2.2:
The semi-quantitative Benedict's test and serial dilutions

In this investigation, you will produce a range of dilutions of glucose by **serial dilution** and use a **semi-quantitative test**, the Benedict's test, to estimate the concentration of a solution of glucose.

YOU WILL NEED

Equipment:
- nine test tubes • test-tube rack • pipettes, 1 cm³ and 10 cm³, and pipette fillers • 50 cm³ of glucose solution, 10% concentration • 20 cm³ of glucose solution, unknown concentration • distilled water, 100 cm³ • Benedict's solution, 100 cm³ • beaker, 50 cm³, 500 cm³ • Bunsen burner, tripod, gauze, heat-proof tile • test-tube holder

Safety considerations

- Make sure you have read the Safety advice section at the beginning of this book and listen to any advice from your teacher before carrying out this investigation.
- If you splash your skin, wash with water.
- Use Bunsen burners with care and tie back long hair.

Method

Part 1: Preparing the different concentrations of glucose by serial dilution

It is important to be able to understand how to make different concentrations of solution by using the technique of serial dilution (Figure 2.2 shows the beginning of this process).

1 Label the test tubes 1–7.

2 Using a pipette, place 10 cm³ 10% glucose solution into tube 1.

3 Remove 1 cm³ of this solution from tube 1 and place into tube 2.

4 Add 9 cm³ distilled water to tube 2 and mix. This is now diluted to 1% glucose.

5 Remove 1 cm³ of the 1% glucose solution from tube 2 and place into tube 3.

6 Add 9 cm³ distilled water into tube 3 and mix. This is now diluted to 0.1% glucose.

7 Remove 1 cm³ of 0.1% glucose from tube 3 and place into tube 4.

8 Add 9 cm³ distilled water to tube 4 and mix. This is now diluted to 0.01% glucose.

9 Remove 1 cm³ of 0.01% glucose from tube 4 and place into tube 5.

10 Add 9 cm³ distilled water to tube 5 and mix. This is now diluted to 0.001% glucose.

11 Remove 1 cm³ of 0.001% glucose from tube 5 and place into tube 6.

12 Place 9 cm³ distilled water into tube 6.

13 Remove 1 cm³ of 0.001% glucose from tube 6 and throw it away.

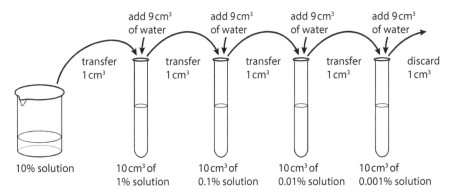

Figure 2.2: Method for serial dilution.

Part 2: Carrying out the Benedict's test

1 Set up a boiling water bath as shown in Practical Investigation 2.1.

2 Place 9 cm³ unknown glucose solution into tube 7.

3 Add 5 cm³ Benedict's solution to each of tubes 1–6.

4 Carefully place tubes 1–6 into the boiling water bath for exactly 5 min.

5 Turn off the Bunsen burner and using a test tube holder, carefully remove the test tubes and place them in a rack in order 1–6.

6 Record the colours of the test tube by either taking a photograph of the rack and sticking it in this workbook, or colouring the test tubes in Figure 2.3 in the Results section below the appropriate colours.

7 Compare the colour of the 'unknown' solution with the colours of the known standards. Identify the concentration of the standards which have the most similar colour. If the colour is not exactly the same as the standard, look at the colours of the solutions with higher and lower concentrations. This can help you to suggest a range within which the concentration lies.

Results

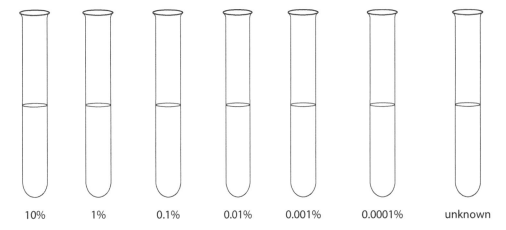

Figure 2.3: Experimental results for investigation 2.2.

Analysis, conclusion and evaluation

a The concentration of glucose in the 'unknown' solution is approximately
........................%. It may lie within a range of ....% to
..................%.

b Explain why this test is considered a semi-quantitative test rather than a
quantitative one.

....

....

....

c How certain can we be about the exact concentration of glucose in the unknown
solution?

....

....

....

d Why was $1\,cm^3$ thrown away from the last dilution?

....

....

....

e Several variables were kept constant for all the tubes. List as many of these
standardised variables as possible and explain why it is essential to keep them
constant.

....

....

....

....

....

f It is important that the amount of Benedict's solution added is greater than the glucose.
Explain how it could affect the result if there were too little Benedict's solution.

....

....

....

g Explain the purpose of tube 6.

....

....

....

h Suggest an alternative method that could be used to make the test fully quantitative.

....

....

....

i Serial dilution can be used to make many different concentration ranges. This experiment used a dilution factor of 10 each time. Calculate the concentrations of glucose solutions that would have been produced if $5\,cm^3$ of water and $5\,cm^3$ glucose solution were used each time instead of $9\,cm^3$ water and $1\,cm^3$ glucose solution.

....

....

....

Practical Investigation 2.3: Using a semi-quantitative iodine test to compare the starch content of bananas

In this investigation, you will make a series of standard starch concentrations by diluting a stock, observe if different starch concentrations give a different colour with iodine solution, and compare the starch content of bananas of different ripeness.

YOU WILL NEED

Equipment:
- nine test tubes • test-tube racks • iodine solution in a dropper bottle
- 1% starch suspension, $50\,cm^3$ • distilled water, $100\,cm^3$ • pipettes, $10\,cm^3$, $1\,cm^3$, pipette filler • pieces of banana flesh from green, yellow and black bananas • knife or scalpel • Bunsen burner, tripod, gauze, heatproof tile
- test-tube holder • glass beakers, $500\,cm^3$ and $50\,cm^3$ • spatula

Safety considerations

- Make sure you have read the Safety advice section at the beginning of this book and listen to any advice from your teacher before carrying out this investigation.

- If you splash your skin, wash with water.

- Use Bunsen burners with care and tie back long hair.

- Care should be taken when working with sharp blades.

- Iodine solution should not be thrown away in water that could come into contact with aquatic life.

Method

Part 1: Making the standard concentrations of starch

1   In Practical Investigation 2.2, you made serial dilutions of glucose. Use the same method to make $9\,cm^3$ of each of the following concentrations of starch suspensions starting with a 1% stock:

- 1%

- 0.1%

- 0.01%

- 0.001%

- 0.0001%

Label each of the five test tubes appropriately.

2   Place $9\,cm^3$ distilled water into a sixth test tube.

3   Add three drops of iodine solution to each tube and mix.

4   Put all the test tubes into a rack in order of decreasing starch concentration.

5   Either colour each tube the appropriate colour in Figure 2.5 in the Results section or take a photograph of the tubes and stick it into this workbook.

Part 2: Making the banana extracts

1   Label three test tubes, A, B and C.

2   Use a knife to cut out a $1\,cm^3$ piece of green, unripe banana (without the peel) and place it into a beaker (see Figure 2.4).

3   Add $10\,cm^3$ distilled water to the beaker and mash the banana with a spatula to make a suspension of banana. Transfer the extract to tube A.

4   Repeat the procedure for the yellow (ripe) and black (over-ripe) bananas, transferring the extracts into tubes B and C respectively.

5   Place all three test tubes into a boiling water bath for 5 min.

6   Remove the tubes from the water bath and leave to cool for 10 min.

7   Add five drops of iodine to each solution, mix and compare each with the standard dilutions.

8 Record the approximate concentrations of starch in each type of banana in the Results section.

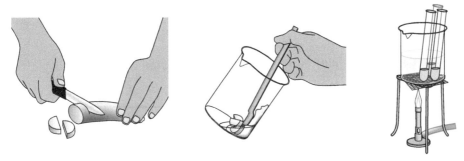

Figure 2.4: Method for Part 2 of investigation 2.3.

Results

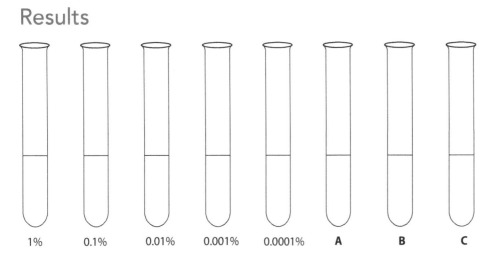

| 1% | 0.1% | 0.01% | 0.001% | 0.0001% | **A** | **B** | **C** |

Figure 2.5: Experimental results for investigation 2.3.

Analysis, conclusion and evaluation

a The approximate starch concentrations and approximate ranges (the concentrations of the standards within which the colour lies) for each banana are:

- green (unripe): concentration............ range: .... to ....

- yellow (ripe): concentration............ range: .... to ....

- black (over-ripe): concentration............ range: .... to ....

b Explain what the investigation shows you about what happens to bananas as they ripen.

....

....

c   Discuss the accuracy of this method and suggest how it could be improved to give more precise values of starch concentrations.

....

....

....

d   Describe four limitations of this investigation. These should not simply be errors but things that mean that the results may not be accurate or the conclusion valid.

1   ....

2   ....

3   ....

4   ....

> **TIP**
>
> Don't confuse limitations with errors. Errors can be the results of limitations of techniques or equipment.

> Chapter 3
Enzymes

CHAPTER OUTLINE

This chapter relates to Chapter 3: Enzymes, in the Coursebook.

In this chapter, you will complete practical investigations on:

- 3.1 The time-course of an enzyme-catalysed reaction
- 3.2 The effect of substrate concentration on the rate of an enzyme-catalysed reaction
- 3.3 The effect of enzyme concentration on the rate of an enzyme-catalysed reaction
- 3.4 The effect of temperature on the rate of an enzyme-catalysed reaction
- 3.5 Immobilising urease
- 3.6 Investigating the effect of an inhibitor on the action of bromelain

Practical Investigation 3.1: The time-course of an enzyme-catalysed reaction

Enzymes are proteins that act as catalysts. They increase the rate of a reaction, but are not changed themselves.

In this investigation, you will measure the rate of reaction by measuring the rate of formation of the product. You will investigate how this changes as the reaction takes place.

The enzyme you are using is catalase. This enzyme catalyses the breakdown of hydrogen peroxide to water and oxygen:

$$\text{hydrogen peroxide} \rightarrow \text{water} + \text{oxygen}$$

$$2H_2O_2 \rightarrow 2H_2O + O_2$$

Hydrogen peroxide is the substrate in this reaction, and water and oxygen are the products.

Catalase is found in almost all living cells. In this investigation, you will **macerate** celery stalks in water. This will break up the cells, so the catalase inside them dissolves in the water.

KEY WORD

macerate: to break something up in water

YOU WILL NEED

Equipment:

• two or three large stalks of celery • about 20 cm³ of 10 volume hydrogen peroxide solution • an electric blender • a filter funnel and muslin • two 250 cm³ beakers • a large test tube, preferably a side-arm test tube • a gas syringe • tubing to make an airtight connection between the test tube and the gas syringe • a timer (e.g. on a phone) • a retort stand, boss and clamp • apparatus for measuring small volumes, for example two 5 cm³ or 10 cm³ syringes or two graduated pipettes

Access to:

• distilled water

Safety considerations

- Make sure you have read the Safety advice section at the beginning of this book and listen to any advice from your teacher before carrying out this investigation.

- Hydrogen peroxide is a strong **oxidising agent** and bleach. Wear safety glasses throughout this practical. If you get hydrogen peroxide on your skin, wash with plenty of cold water.

- If oxygen is given off very quickly, the plunger of the syringe may move so fast that it shoots out of the end of the syringe and could hit someone. You can avoid this by tying the plunger loosely to the syringe with a piece of string.

Method

Part 1: Preliminary work

You are going to decide suitable concentrations of the enzyme and substrate to use when carrying out the main part of the investigation. This is difficult to predict, because you do not know how much catalase the celery contains, nor how fast the enzyme will work.

1   Break or cut one or two large stalks of celery into several pieces and place in an electric blender. Add approximately 400 cm³ of distilled water. (Make a note of the mass of celery and the volume of water that you use, as this may be helpful later.) Switch on the blender to make a **suspension** of celery extract in water.

2   Place some muslin in a filter funnel, and support the funnel over a beaker. Pour the celery extract into the funnel, and leave it so the liquid part of the extract passes through the muslin. You can squeeze it gently to speed up this process.

3   Connect a large, side-arm test tube to a gas syringe. Check that the plunger of the gas syringe moves freely. Support the test tube and gas syringe using a retort stand, boss and clamp.

KEY WORDS

oxidising agent: a substance that removes electrons from another substance

suspension: a mixture of a solid substance and a liquid, where small particles of the solid float in the liquid, but do not dissolve

TIP

Any biological material will contain catalase. If celery is not available, try other plant material, such as potato, carrot, apple or other fruit or vegetable.

Figure 3.1 also shows an alternative arrangement, if you do not have a side-arm test tube.

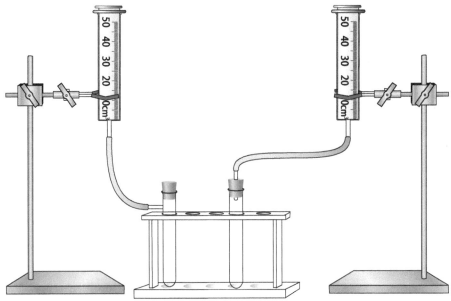

Figure 3.1: Apparatus for part 1 of investigation 3.1.

4   Measure 20 cm³ of hydrogen peroxide solution and place in the test tube.

5   Measure 5 cm³ of celery extract.

6   Add the celery extract to the hydrogen peroxide solution, and replace the bung as quickly as you can.

7   As oxygen is given off, the plunger of the gas syringe will move. Note how quickly this moves, and decide whether you will be able to measure the volume of oxygen in the syringe at 15 s or 30 s intervals. If the reaction is too fast for you to do this, consider how you can change the volume of either hydrogen peroxide or celery extract to slow it down. (It is unlikely that the reaction will be too slow, but if this happens try making a new celery extract using more celery and less water.)

8   Repeat Steps 4–7, trying different concentrations or volumes of enzyme or celery extract, until you are confident that you will be able to take readings of the volume of oxygen in the syringe at 15 s or 30 s intervals.

Part 2: Measuring the rate of oxygen formation over time

1   Ensure that your apparatus is completely clean and air-tight, with the gas syringe reading 0.

2   Add the required volume of hydrogen peroxide solution to the test tube.

3   Add the required volume of celery extract to the hydrogen peroxide in the tube. *Immediately* push the bung into the tube and start the timer.

4   Record the volume of oxygen in the gas syringe every 15 s or 30 s, in Table 3.1. Add more rows to the results table as required. Continue until the rate of oxygen production starts to remain the same.

Results

Time / s	Volume of oxygen / cm³

> **TIP**
>
> Think about the degree of precision with which you can read the volumes. This will depend on the scale on the gas syringe. For example, if it is marked off in cm³, you can probably read the scale to the nearest 0.5 cm³.

Table 3.1: Results table for part 2 of investigation 3.1.

Analysis, conclusion and evaluation

a   On the following grid, plot a line graph with Time / s on the *x*-axis and Volume of oxygen / cm³ on the *y*-axis.

Take care to:

- use most of the graph paper

- use a scale on the *x*-axis that runs from 0 to your longest time measured

- use a scale on the *x*-axis that goes up in sensible, equal intervals, for example 15 or 30 s

- use a scale on the *y*-axis that runs from 0 to just above the greatest volume that you measured

- use a scale on the *y*-axis that goes up in sensible, equal intervals

- plot points with a very small, neat, carefully placed cross (x not +)

- draw a smooth **best-fit line**.

> **KEY WORD**
>
> **best-fit line:** a smooth line which shows the trend that the points seem to fit. There is not a single perfect place to put a best-fit line, but you should ensure that approximately the same number of points, roughly the same distances from the line, lie above and below its initial rate of reaction

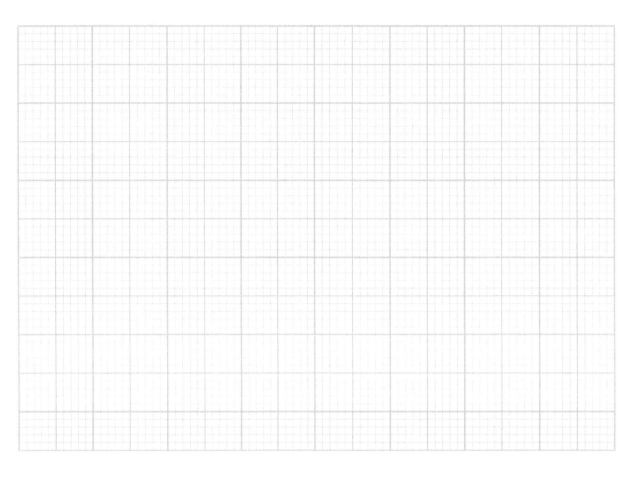

b The steeper the slope (gradient) of the line, the greater the rate of the reaction. Describe how the rate of the reaction changes with time.

....

....

....

> **TIP**
>
> Remember that 'describe' means you simply write what you can see, without trying to say *why* the rate of reaction changes in this way.

c On your graph, at what time is the concentration of substrate greatest? Explain your answer.

....

....

d On your graph, at what time has all of the substrate been converted to product? Explain your answer.

....

....

e Use your answers to **b**, **c** and **d** to explain the shape of the curve.

....

....

....

....

....

f You are now going to use your graph to find the **initial rate of reaction**. This is the rate of reaction as close to the start as you can measure.

- Draw a tangent to your curve as close to the origin as possible, perhaps at around 10, 20 or 15 s. Your tangent must be at least half as long as the line of the graph, so make it as long as possible (see Figure 3.2).

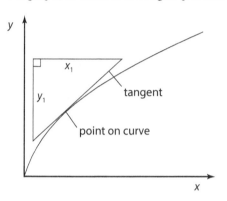

Figure 3.2: Calculating the initial rate of reaction.

- Draw a right-angled triangle, with the tangent as the hypotenuse.

- Measure the lengths of x_1 and y_1. Use the scales on the x-axis and y-axis to record these as seconds and cm³ of oxygen, respectively.

$x_1 = $ .... s

$y_1 = $ .... cm³ of oxygen

- Calculate the gradient, by dividing y_1 by x_1. This gives you the initial rate of reaction in cm³ of oxygen per second.

....

....

g   In most enzyme investigations, you will want to find out the effect of a variable (e.g. substrate concentration, or temperature) on the rate of the reaction. You will need to keep all other variables constant.

Using your answers to **c** and **d**, explain why it is important to measure the rate of reaction as close to the start of the reaction as possible.

....

....

....

h   This method involves several important sources of experimental error (uncertainty), which means we cannot be sure that we would get exactly the same results if we did the experiment again.

For each of the following sources of error listed, decide:

- whether it is a **random error** or a **systematic error**

- how it is likely to affect the results.

The first one has been done for you.

i   The apparatus may not have been completely airtight.

systematic error: some gas may have escaped, so the volume of oxygen measured would be too small and the rate of the reaction would seem slower than it really was.

ii   The bung may not have been placed into the test tube fast enough.

....

....

iii   The readings may not have been taken at exactly correct time intervals.

....

....

iv   The scale on the gas syringe may not have been totally accurate.

....

....

v   It is difficult to decide exactly how to draw the tangent on the curve.

....

....

TIP

Sources of error can be **random errors**, where the size and direction of the error are not always the same. This can happen when a variable that should be kept constant changes unpredictably. For example, the temperature of the room might change, which could affect the result of the reaction. **Systematic errors** are where the size and direction of the error is relatively constant. This can happen if a piece of apparatus is wrongly calibrated, or if there is a fault in the equipment that always makes your measurements larger or smaller than they should be.

KEY WORDS

random error: a source of uncertainty in your results that gives incorrect values that can be of different magnitudes; random errors can affect trends shown by results

systematic error: a source of uncertainty in your results that gives incorrect values that are always of the same magnitude; systematic errors do not affect trends shown by results

Practical Investigation 3.2: The effect of substrate concentration on the rate of an enzyme-catalysed reaction

In Practical Investigation 3.1, you measured the initial rate of reaction for the breakdown of hydrogen peroxide, catalysed by the enzyme catalase. In this practical, you use the same reaction and method to investigate how changing the concentration of the substrate affects the initial rate of reaction.

In this investigation:

- the **independent variable** (the one you change) is the concentration of the substrate, hydrogen peroxide

- the **dependent variable** is the rate at which oxygen is produced.

YOU WILL NEED

Equipment:

- two or three large stalks of celery • about 100 cm³ of 10 volume hydrogen peroxide solution • an electric blender • a filter funnel and muslin • two 250 cm³ beakers • five 100 cm³ beakers or other small containers • method of labelling beakers, for example glass marker pen • a large test tube • a gas syringe • tubing to make an airtight connection between the test tube and the gas syringe • a timer (e.g. on a phone) • a retort stand, boss and clamp • apparatus for measuring small volumes, for example two 5 cm³ or 10 cm³ syringes or two graduated pipettes

Access to:

- distilled water

KEY WORDS

independent variable: the variable (factor) that is deliberately changed in an experiment

dependent variable: the variable that the experiment is measuring (and that changes as a result of changing the independent variable)

Safety considerations

- Make sure you have read the Safety advice section at the beginning of this book and listen to any advice from your teacher before carrying out this investigation.

- Hydrogen peroxide is a strong oxidising agent and bleach. Wear safety glasses throughout this practical. If you get hydrogen peroxide on your skin, wash with plenty of cold water.

TIP

Any biological material will contain catalase. If celery is not available, try other plant material such as potato, carrot, apple or other fruit or vegetables.

Method

1 Set up the apparatus as in Practical Investigation 3.1.

2 Make up a celery extract as in Practical Investigation 3.1. It will be helpful if you can use celery from a similar source, and in similar quantities, because you know that this produces a measurable rate of reaction.

3 Use dilution to produce a range of concentrations of hydrogen peroxide solution. You could try 100, 80, 60, 40 and 20% of the concentration of the original solution.

Use the space here to construct a table showing how you prepared the different concentrations.

> **TIP**
>
> See Practical Investigation 2.3 to help you to design the table. You may also like to refer to the Cambridge AS & A Level Biology Coursebook.

4 Read Steps 5–6, and then construct a results table in the space overleaf. You can use a similar design to the one in Practical Investigation 3.1, but with extra columns for the different concentrations of substrate.

5 Using your highest concentration of hydrogen peroxide, measure and record the volume of oxygen produced over time, exactly as you did in Practical Investigation 3.1.

6 Repeat for each concentration of hydrogen peroxide solution.

Results

Take care to:

- draw the table using a ruler

- include full headings for each column, including units – do not include units with the individual readings

- write each reading to the same number of decimal places.

Analysis, conclusion and evaluation

a   On the grid, plot curves for each of the concentrations of hydrogen peroxide.
Draw a best-fit line for each set of data.

Note: if you prefer, you can use separate sheets of graph paper to plot separate
graphs for each concentration. If you do this, use the same scales for each graph.

b Use the curves to calculate the initial rate of reaction for each concentration of hydrogen peroxide.

Record your calculated results in Table 3.2.

Substrate concentration / percentage of original solution	Initial rate of reaction / cm³ of oxygen s⁻¹

Table 3.2: Calculated results.

c Use the results from Table 3.2 to plot a graph of initial rate of reaction against substrate concentration. Draw a smooth best-fit curve.

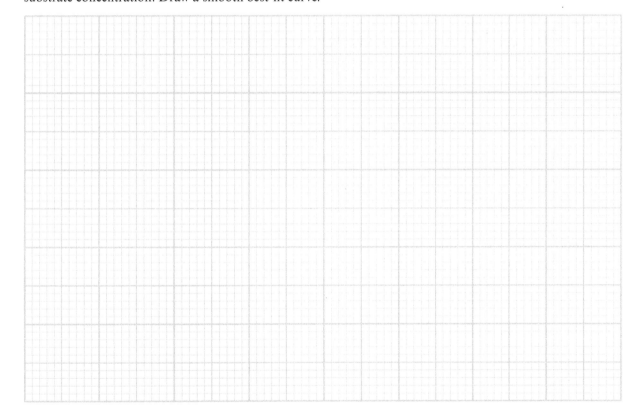

d Identify any values that do not fit the pattern shown by the other results. These are anomalous results.

e   Use your results to write a brief conclusion about how the concentration of substrate affects the initial rate of reaction.

....

....

....

....

f   Using your knowledge of how enzymes catalyse reactions, explain the reasons for the relationship that you have described in your answer to question **e**.

....

....

....

....

g   List **four** significant sources of error that reduce the reliability of your results.
    At least **two** of these sources of error should be different from those listed in Practical Investigation 3.1.

....

....

....

....

....

h   Select **two** of the sources of error that you have listed.
    For each one, suggest how you could adapt the method to reduce this error.

....

....

....

....

....

Practical Investigation 3.3: The effect of enzyme concentration on the rate of an enzyme-catalysed reaction

In this investigation, you will use the enzyme amylase, which catalyses the hydrolysis of starch to maltose. Amylase is produced by many different organisms, including humans, some bacteria and some fungi.

In Practical Investigations 3.1 and 3.2, you measured the rate of reaction by measuring the rate of formation of the product, oxygen. In this investigation, you will measure the rate of reaction by measuring the rate of disappearance of the substrate.

The reaction is:

starch → maltose + water

YOU WILL NEED

Equipment:
- about 50 cm³ of a 1% solution of amylase (or as supplied by your teacher)
- about 50 cm³ of a 5% solution of starch (or as supplied by your teacher)
- two 250 cm³ beakers • five 100 cm³ beakers or other small containers
- method of labelling beakers, for example glass marker pen • at least 12 clean test tubes • six glass rods • a timer (e.g. on a phone) • apparatus for measuring small volumes, e.g. two 5 cm³ or 10 cm³ syringes or two graduated pipettes • iodine in potassium iodide solution, with a dropper • two white tiles, preferably with a series of hollows (a spotting tile or dimple tile)
- starch-free paper for cleaning the glass rods

Access to:
- distilled water • a thermostatically controlled water bath, or apparatus to make your own

Safety considerations

- Make sure you have read the Safety advice section at the beginning of this book and listen to any advice from your teacher before carrying out this investigation.

- If you get iodine in potassium iodide solution on your skin, wash it immediately with plenty of cold water.

Method

1   You are provided with a 1% solution of amylase. Use dilution to make up a range of four more concentrations of amylase: 0.8, 0.6, 0.4 and 0.2%.

    Construct a table in the following space to show how you will do this.

2 Label six clean test tubes with the concentration of amylase that you will place in each one. One of them should contain no amylase.

3 Measure 5 cm³ of each of your amylase solutions into each of five labelled test tubes. Measure 5 cm³ of distilled water into the sixth tube. Wash the pipette or syringe between each solution, or use a different one for each. Stand all the tubes in a water bath set at 40 °C.

4 Measure 5 cm³ of starch suspension into six more test tubes. Stand all the tubes in the same water bath.

5 Leave all the tubes to stand for at least 10 min, to allow the temperature of their contents to come to the same temperature as the water bath. After 10 min, check these temperatures with a thermometer. Wash and dry the thermometer between each measurement, to avoid contaminating one tube with the contents of another. If necessary, leave the tubes for longer.

6 While you are waiting, prepare the spotting tiles.

- Label the tiles with the concentrations of enzyme you are testing.

- Place spots of iodine in potassium iodide solution onto the spotting tile or tiles. Arrange them in five rows, as shown in Figure 3.3.

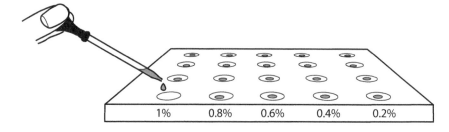

Figure 3.3: Method for adding iodine onto a spotting tile.

7   When you are satisfied that the contents of all of the tubes are at the correct temperature, dip a glass rod into one of the suspensions and then dip the rod into the first spot of iodine solution on the 1% row on the tile. Wipe or wash the glass rod clean.

8   Tip one of the starch suspensions into the tube containing 1% starch suspension. Immediately stir with a glass rod and start the timer.

9   Take samples from the mixture every minute (or as advised by your teacher) and add them to the next spot of iodine solution on the tile. Do this by dipping a clean glass rod into the reacting mixture, and then immediately dipping the rod into the iodine solution.

10 Continue until the iodine solution remains orange–brown, or after 15 min (whichever is sooner).

11 Repeat Steps 7–9 for each of the other concentrations of enzyme.

12 Record your results in Table 3.3.

> **TIP**
>
> Glass rods that are not cleaned properly can completely spoil your experiment, by transferring amylase or starch from one tube or iodine spot to another. Note that paper towels often contain starch, so check this before you use them. If you do not have any starch-free paper, then wash the rod in absolutely clean water each time.

Results

Concentration of enzyme solution / %	Time taken for starch to disappear / s

Table 3.3: Results table.

Analysis, conclusion and evaluation

a   Add a third column to Table 3.3.

Calculate the rate of reaction for each concentration of enzyme.

$$rate = 1 \div time$$

Multiply this number by 1000, and give your answer to one decimal place.

Add your calculated values to the third column in the results table. Remember to add a suitable heading for this column.

b   On the grid, plot a graph of rate of reaction against concentration of enzyme.

Join the points with ruled straight lines.

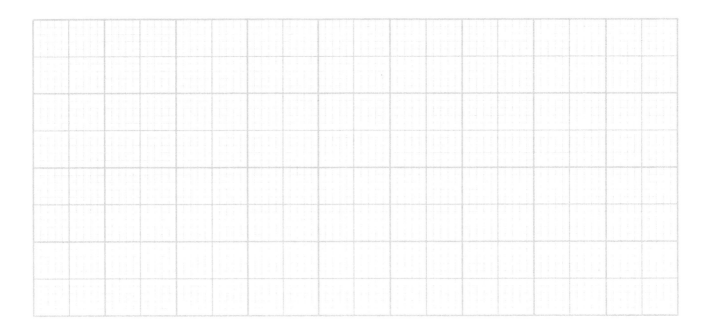

c Write a brief conclusion for your experiment.

....

....

....

....

d Using your knowledge and understanding of how enzymes work, explain your results. Use these terms in your explanation:

active site   enzyme–substrate complex

....

....

....

....

....

e   When investigating the effect of one variable (the independent variable) on another (the dependent variable), it is important to keep all other variables that might affect the independent variable the same.

These are called **standardised variables**.

List **two** important standardised variables in this investigation.

....

....

f   Identify **three** important sources of experimental error in your investigation, which reduce the confidence that you have in your results and conclusion.

....

....

....

g   Select **two** of the sources of error in your answer to **f** above. For each of these, suggest how you could adapt the method to reduce the source of error. Assume that you would have as much time as you need, and any other apparatus that you would require.

....

....

....

....

....

....

h   Apart from reducing the sources of error, suggest **one** other way in which the investigation could be improved.

....

....

i   Explain why you measured the time taken for disappearance of substrate to measure the rate of reaction in this experiment, whereas for the catalase reaction you measured the volume of oxygen produced over time.

....

....

....

....

Practical Investigation 3.4: The effect of temperature on the rate of an enzyme-catalysed reaction

In this investigation, you will again investigate the reaction in which catalase catalyses the breakdown of hydrogen peroxide.

This time, you will find out how varying the temperature affects the rate of reaction.

You are going to plan part of this investigation yourself.

YOU WILL NEED

Equipment:
• one or two stalks of celery • about 100 cm³ of 10 volume hydrogen peroxide solution • an electric blender or pestle and mortar • a filter funnel and muslin (fine cloth that can be used for filtering) • two 250 cm³ beakers • five 100 cm³ beakers or other small containers • method of labelling beakers, for example glass marker pen • a large test tube • a gas syringe • tubing to make an airtight connection between the test tube and the gas syringe • a timer (e.g. on a phone) • a retort stand, boss and clamp • apparatus for measuring small volumes, for example two 5 cm³ or 10 cm³ syringes or two graduated pipettes

Access to:
• distilled water
• several thermostatically controlled water baths, and/or apparatus to make your own water baths using large beakers of water

---

Safety considerations

• Make sure you have read the Safety advice section at the beginning of this book and listen to any advice from your teacher before carrying out this investigation.

• Hydrogen peroxide is a strong oxidising agent and bleach. Wear safety glasses throughout this practical. If you get hydrogen peroxide on your skin, wash with plenty of cold water.

Method

For this investigation, you can use the same technique as the one described in Practical 3.1.

1   The independent variable in this investigation is temperature.

Decide on the **range** of the independent variable. The range is the spread between the lowest temperature and the highest temperature that you will investigate.

Range for the independent variable will be ....

KEY WORD

range: the spread between the lowest and highest value

2 You should have at least five values for your independent variable.

Write down what these values will be.

....

3 How you change the independent variable will depend on the apparatus that is available to you. Use thermostatically controlled water baths if you can. Otherwise, you can make water baths using large beakers, ice and a source of hot water.

Describe how you will change and measure the independent variable. Think about how you will make sure that the mixture of enzyme and substrate really is at the temperature you want it to be.

....

....

....

....

4 The dependent variable in this investigation is the rate of reaction.

If you had time, you could measure and calculate the initial rate of reaction for each value of your independent variable, as you did in Practical Investigation 3.2. However, to save time in this investigation, you can simply measure the volume of oxygen produced in a chosen time period.

Describe how you will measure your dependent variable.

....

....

....

....

....

5 All other variables that could affect the rate of the reaction must be kept the same. These are called standardised variables.

List **two** standardised variables.

For each one, explain how you will keep it constant.

standardised variable 1 ....

standardised variable 2 ....

6   Construct a results table in the Results section on the next page.

7   Carry out your method.

Use the following space to describe your method. There is no need to describe the technique in detail where it is the same as in Practical Investigation 3.1.

....

....

....

....

....

....

....

....

....

....

....

....

....

....

Results

Construct your results table in the following space.

Put the independent variable in the first column, and the dependent variable in the second column.

Remember to make all your readings to the same number of decimal places.

Analysis, conclusion and evaluation

a   Draw a graph on the following grid.
    Join the points with ruled, straight lines.

b   Write a short, clear conclusion, describing how temperature affects the rate of this
    reaction.

    ....

    ....

    ....

c Using your knowledge and understanding of how enzymes function, explain your results.

....

....

....

....

d Describe how you could carry out a further investigation to determine the optimum temperature more precisely.

....

....

....

....

e Describe how you could use a similar method to investigate the effect of pH on the activity of catalase. pH can be altered by using different **buffer solutions**.

....

....

....

....

....

....

....

....

....

....

....

KEY WORD
buffer solution: a solution that has a known pH, which can be added to a reacting mixture to maintain the pH at that level

Practical Investigation 3.5:
Immobilising urease

In industry, immobilised enzymes are widely used because they are more stable than in liquid solution, and because they do not contaminate the product.

In this investigation, you will use the enzyme urease. This enzyme catalyses the decomposition of urea into carbon dioxide and ammonia.

You are going to immobilise the enzyme. You will do this by trapping it inside beads of calcium alginate, which forms a jelly.

Ammonia forms an alkaline solution. You will measure the production of ammonia by monitoring the change in pH.

YOU WILL NEED

Equipment:

- about $50 \, cm^3$ of 0.6% urease solution • about $100 \, cm^3$ of 2% urea solution
- a $20 \, cm^3$ syringe barrel, with a short length of rubber tubing attached to its nozzle • a clamp to hold the tubing closed • a retort stand, boss and clamp to support the syringe barrel • a small piece of muslin • a tea strainer
- several glass beakers (small or medium size) • about $80 \, cm^3$ of 3% sodium alginate solution • about $100 \, cm^3$ of 3% calcium chloride solution • a timer (e.g. on a phone) • apparatus for measuring small volumes, for example two $5 \, cm^3$ or $10 \, cm^3$ syringes or two graduated pipettes • a pH meter and probe
- a dropper pipette with a fine nozzle

Access to:

- distilled water

Safety considerations

- Make sure you have read the Safety advice section at the beginning of this book and listen to any advice from your teacher before carrying out this investigation.

- Urease, like all enzymes, can irritate skin. Wash immediately with plenty of cold water if you get any on your skin.

Method

1 Cut a small piece of muslin, and push it into the syringe to cover the entrance to the nozzle. (This will prevent the beads of calcium alginate getting into the nozzle.)

2   Support the syringe barrel, nozzle downwards, in a clamp (Figure 3.4).

You are now going to immobilise the enzyme by trapping it in jelly beads.

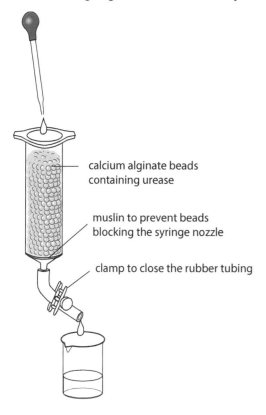

calcium alginate beads
containing urease

muslin to prevent beads
blocking the syringe nozzle

clamp to close the rubber tubing

Figure 3.4: Apparatus for investigation 3.5.

3   Measure 50 cm³ of sodium alginate solution into a medium-sized beaker. Add 50 cm³ of urease solution and mix thoroughly.

4   Using a dropper pipette with a fine nozzle, add a small drop of urea–sodium alginate solution to the calcium chloride. The calcium chloride and sodium alginate will react to produce calcium alginate, which forms a bead of jelly. Urease molecules will be trapped inside the jelly bead.

5   Repeat Step 4 many times, to produce as many jelly beads as you can. You need enough to fill the barrel of the syringe that you have supported in the clamp.

6   Carefully collect the beads (do not break them up) into the tea strainer, and wash gently using distilled water (Figure 3.5).

calcium alginate beads

tea strainer

Figure 3.5: Washing alginate beads.

7   Place the beads inside the syringe barrel. Very gently push them together, or tap the syringe barrel, to reduce any large gaps between them.

8   Place a clean beaker underneath the syringe barrel.

9   Use the pH meter to measure the pH of the urea solution, and record it in a suitable table in the space in the Results section.

10   Partially open the clamp on the rubber tubing. Slowly pour the urea solution into the top of the syringe barrel, so that it flows slowly down over the beads and out through the nozzle of the syringe, into the beaker. You can adjust the speed at which it moves through the beads by loosening or tightening the clamp on the rubber tubing.

11   Measure the pH of the liquid in the beaker and record it.

Results

Analysis, conclusion and evaluation

a   Explain your results.

....

....

....

....

....

b   You could check if the solution in the beaker still contains any urea using the following method:

   •   Put some of the solution into a small beaker.

   •   Place some beads containing immobilised urease into the solution in the beaker.

   •   If the solution contains urea, the urease in the beads will break it down and release carbon dioxide. (If there is enough carbon dioxide, the bubbles that stick to the beads may cause them to float to the surface.)

   Describe and explain your results.

....

....

....

c   Suggest how you could use the techniques in this investigation, and the techniques that you used in Practical Investigation 3.4, to test this hypothesis:

   immobilised urease denatures at a higher temperature than urease in free solution.

....

....

....

....

....

....

....

....

....

....

....

....

....

....

Practical Investigation 3.6 Investigating the effect of an inhibitor on the action of bromelain

In this investigation, you will investigate the effect of copper ions on the activity of a protease enzyme, bromelain, found in fresh pineapple. This enzyme hydrolyses proteins – in this case, gelatin – to soluble amino acids.

YOU WILL NEED

Equipment:

• about 50 cm³ of an extract made from fresh pineapple • a small quantity of boiled pineapple extract • five small Petri dishes containing coloured jelly, made using gelatin • about 10 cm³ of 1 mol dm⁻³ copper sulfate solution • a cork borer • a ruler to measure in mm

Safety considerations

• Make sure you have read the Safety advice section at the beginning of this book and listen to any advice from your teacher before carrying out this investigation.

• If you get copper sulfate solution on your skin, wash immediately with cold water.

Method

1 You are provided with $1\,mol\,dm^{-3}$ copper sulfate solution. Use this solution to make up $10\,cm^3$ each of solutions of 0.1, 0.01 and $0.001\,mol\,dm^{-3}$.

Describe how you will do this. You can do this in words, or present your results in a table.

2 Use a cork borer to cut one small, neat well in the agar jelly near the centre of each Petri dish (Figure 3.6). Try not to touch the rest of the jelly with your fingers as you do this.

jelly containing protein

well cut with cork borer

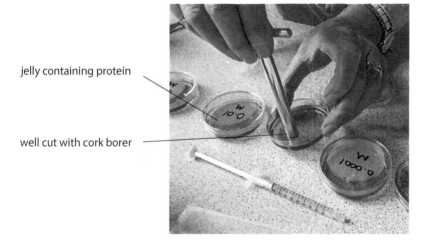

Figure 3.6: Method for cutting a well in agar jelly.

3 Using small syringes, add the same total volume of liquid (determine how much you think is suitable – it will depend on the depth and diameter of the holes you have made) to each well, as follows:

Petri dish 1: boiled pineapple extract and water

Petri dish 2: fresh pineapple extract and water

Petri dish 3: fresh pineapple extract and $1\,mol\,dm^{-3}$ copper sulfate solution

Petri dish 4: fresh pineapple extract and $0.1 \, mol \, dm^{-3}$ copper sulfate solution

Petri dish 5: fresh pineapple extract and $0.01 \, mol \, dm^{-3}$ copper sulfate solution

Petri dish 6: fresh pineapple extract and $0.001 \, mol \, dm^{-3}$ copper sulfate solution

4 Place lids on each Petri dish, and label them. Leave the dishes for approximately 1 h, or as suggested by your teacher.

5 Use a small pipette to very carefully extract the liquid from the hole in Petri dish 1. Measure the diameter of the well. Repeat for all six dishes. Record your results in a suitable results table here.

Results

Analysis, conclusion and evaluation

a Describe your results.

....

....

....

....

....

b Explain your results.

....

....

....

....

....

....

....

....

c Identify the most significant sources of experimental error in your investigation.

....

....

....

....

....

d Suggest how this investigation could be improved, to give more confidence in your results and conclusion.

....

....

....

....

....

Cell membranes and transport

This chapter relates to Chapter 4: Cell membranes and transport, in the Coursebook.

In this chapter, you will complete practical investigations on:

- 4.1 The effect of salt solutions on eggs

- 4.2 Measuring the rate of osmosis using an osmometer

- 4.3 The effect of surface area : volume ratio on the rate of diffusion

- 4.4 The effect of temperature or concentration gradient on the rate of diffusion

- 4.5 Estimating the water potential of potato tuber cells

- 4.6 Investigating plasmolysis in onion epidermis cells

- 4.7 Determining water potential using density

- 4.8 The effect of temperature on membrane permeability.

Practical Investigation 4.1: The effect of salt solutions on eggs

Underneath the hard shell of a hen's egg, there is a partially permeable membrane. This membrane allows water-molecules to pass through, but not sodium ions or chloride ions.

In this investigation, you will cover hen's eggs in sodium chloride solutions of different concentrations. Water will either enter or leave the egg, by osmosis, through the partially permeable membrane. You can measure how much water has entered or left the egg by measuring changes in mass over time.

YOU WILL NEED

Equipment:

Day 1

- five hen's eggs • a very large beaker to hold all five eggs • a large spoon or other implement for lowering the eggs into the acid • enough 1.5 mol dm⁻³ hydrochloric acid to cover the eggs in the beaker

Day 2

- a large spoon or other implement for removing the eggs from the acid • about 400 cm³ 20% sodium chloride solution • 1 cm³ and 10 cm³ syringes or pipettes • a timer (e.g. on a phone) • 6 × 400 cm³ beakers • paper towel

Access to:

- electronic balance • distilled water

Safety considerations

- Make sure you have read the Safety advice section at the beginning of this book and listen to any advice from your teacher before carrying out this investigation.

- Do not get hydrochloric acid on your skin or clothes. Wash immediately with plenty of cold water if this happens.

- Wear safety glasses.

Method

Part 1: Removing the shells from the eggs and making up salt solutions

The shells of birds' eggs contain calcium carbonate. This reacts with acid to form carbon dioxide and water. Placing the eggs in acid overnight will remove the shells, but will leave the partially permeable membrane underneath undamaged.

1 Place five hen's eggs into a container, for example a large beaker.

2 Pour enough $1.5 \, mol \, dm^{-3}$ hydrochloric acid into the container to completely cover the eggs.

3 Place in a safe place and leave overnight.

4 You are provided with a 20% sodium chloride solution. Complete Table 4.1 and then use your table to make up a range of five different concentrations of sodium chloride solution. You will need to make 200 cm³ of each solution.

Final concentration of solution / %	Volume of sodium chloride solution added / cm³	Volume of distilled water added / cm³
0	0	200
5		
10		
15		
20	200	0

Table 4.1: Results table.

Part 2: Setting up the experiment

1   Carefully remove the hen's eggs, one at a time, from the hydrochloric acid. Wash each egg in water, very gently, and dry using a paper towel. Take care not to break the membrane that surrounds the egg.

2   Measure the mass of each egg in turn, and record these measurements in Table 4.2. Place each egg in a labelled beaker.

3   Start a timer. Pour the different concentrations of salt solution over each egg, making sure that the egg is completely covered.

4   After the eggs have been in their solutions for 30 min, gently remove each egg and dry it. Measure its mass and record this value in Table 4.2.

TIP

You may like to arrange when you pour the solutions over the eggs for different times, so that you do not need to take them out to measure their final mass all at the same time.

Results

Concentration of sodium chloride solution / %	Initial mass of egg / g	Final mass of egg / g	Percentage change in mass

Table 4.2: Results table.

a   Describe any qualitative observations you can make about the eggs in the different solutions, such as their appearance or how they feel to touch.

    ....

    ....

    ....

    ....

Analysis, conclusion and evaluation

a   Calculate the percentage change in mass of each egg. Write your answers in Table 4.2. To calculate percentage change in mass:

   • First find the change in mass by subtracting the final value from the initial value.

   • Then calculate this as a percentage of the initial mass, using this formula:

      percentage change in mass = (change in mass ÷ initial mass) × 100

Show your working.

Write your answer to the same number of decimal places as, or one more than, your original readings for the mass of the eggs.

TIP

Remember always to show each step in your calculations clearly, so that someone else can follow it.

Remember to show whether the percentage in mass is an increase or a decrease.

Note: a percentage does not have any units.

b On the grid, plot a line graph with Concentration of sodium chloride solution / % on the x-axis and Percentage change in mass on the y-axis. Identify any anomalous results and circle them. (You should ignore these points from now on.) Join the points with ruled straight lines.

TIP

Look back at Practical Investigation 3.1 or the Practical skills chapter at the beginning of the book, to remind yourself of the criteria for constructing a good line graph.

c   Describe the effect of sodium chloride solutions on the percentage change in mass of the eggs.

....

....

....

....

....

d   Use your understanding of osmosis to explain your results.

....

....

....

....

....

....

e   State the **two** most important sources of error that you consider may have reduced the reliability of your results.

source of error 1

....

....

source of error 2

....

....

Practical Investigation 4.2: Measuring the rate of osmosis using an osmometer

In this investigation, you will use an artificial partially permeable membrane to separate water from a sucrose solution. You will measure the rate at which water moves into the sucrose solution. You will then plan how you can use this technique to investigate the effect of the water potential gradient on the rate of osmosis.

Safety considerations

- Make sure you have read the Safety advice section at the beginning of this book and listen to any advice from your teacher before carrying out this investigation.

- Take care when handling the glass tubing, in case it has sharp ends.

Part 1: Measuring water movement by osmosis over time

Method

1 Partly fill a 500 cm³ beaker with distilled water.

2 Place a retort stand, boss and clamp next to the beaker. Gently clamp the glass tubing so that the bottom part of it is just inside the beaker. (See Figure 4.1)

3 Cut a piece of Visking tubing about 15 cm long. Moisten it with distilled water and gently rub it with your fingers to soften and open it. Tie a knot in the bottom end of the tubing, to make a tight seal.

4 Fill the tubing with sucrose solution.

5 Hold the filled Visking tubing in the beaker, so that the end of the glass tubing is immersed in the sucrose solution. Tie the top of the Visking tubing very tightly to the glass tubing.

6 If necessary, add more distilled water to the large beaker, so that the Visking tubing is almost entirely covered by the water.

7 Mark the position of the meniscus on the glass tubing.

8 Every 2 min, record the position of the meniscus in a suitable results table, in the Results section.

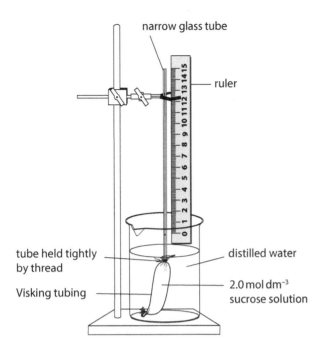

Figure 4.1: Apparatus for Part 1 of investigation 4.2.

Results

Analysis, conclusion and evaluation

a   Display your results as a line graph.

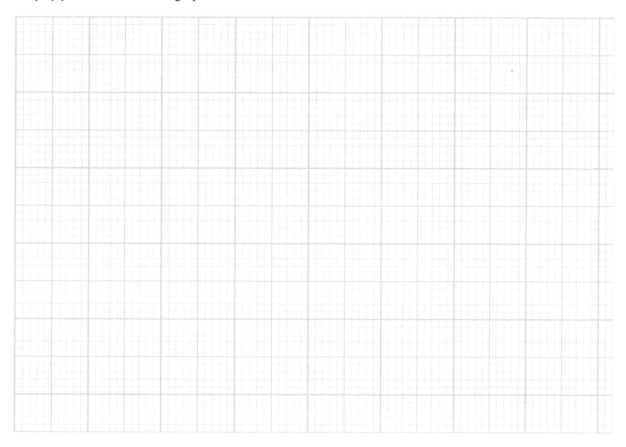

b   Calculate the difference between the original position of the meniscus and the final position of the meniscus. Divide this by the time taken, to find the mean rate of movement of the meniscus.

> **TIP**
>
> Remember to show each step in your working, and to use the correct number of decimal places in your answer.

Part 2: Investigating the effect of water potential gradient on the rate of osmosis

In this part of the investigation, you will vary the concentration of sucrose solution inside the Visking tubing. This will mean that the water potential gradient – the difference in water potential between the water in the beaker and the solution inside the Visking tubing – will vary. You can measure the rate of osmosis by measuring the position of the meniscus after a chosen time.

Method

1   The concentration of sucrose solution is your independent variable in this investigation. Decide how you can use the 2.0 mol dm^{-3} sucrose solution to make up a range of at least five different concentrations of sucrose solutions. (One of them can be 0 – that is, distilled water.) Construct a table in the following space to show how you will do this.

> **TIP**
>
> Remember that a concentrated sucrose solution has a lower water potential than a dilute sucrose solution – that is, a concentrated sucrose solution has a water potential with a more negative value. Distilled water has a water potential of 0.

2   Make up your sucrose solutions. You will need enough of each one to fill a piece of Visking tubing.

3   Describe how and when you will measure your dependent variable in this investigation.

....

....

....

....

4   List **four** variables that you will keep the same in your investigation.

....

....

5   Construct a suitable results chart in the Results section. Then carry out your investigation and record your results in the table.

Results

Analysis, conclusion and evaluation

a   Display your results as a line graph.

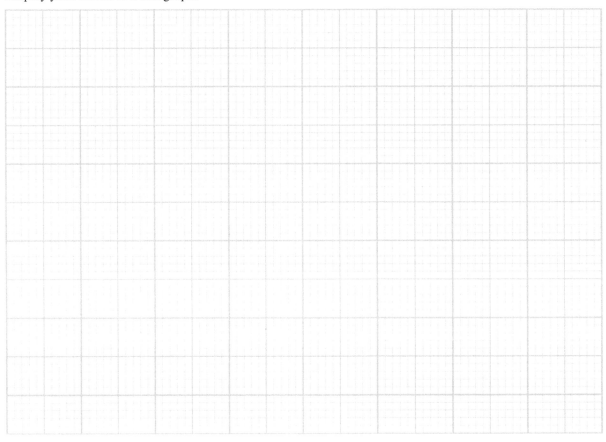

b   Describe the effect of water potential gradient on the rate of osmosis.

....

....

....

....

....

TIP

Remember that the independent variable goes on the *x*-axis, and the dependent variable on the *y*-axis.

c   List **three** significant sources of error that reduce your confidence in your results.

For each source of error, explain whether this is a systematic or random error, and explain how it would affect your results.

source of error 1

....

....

....

source of error 2

....

....

....

source of error 3

....

....

....

Practical Investigation 4.3: The effect of surface area : volume ratio on the rate of diffusion

Many organisms depend on diffusion and osmosis (which is, of course, a type of diffusion) to exchange materials with their environment. The rate at which substances can be exchanged depends on the surface area, while the rate at which substances are used or produced is affected by the number of cells in the organism – that is, its volume. As an organism gets larger, its surface area increases less than its volume increases. Large organisms therefore have smaller surface area : volume ratios than small organisms.

In this investigation, you will use pieces of agar jelly to represent organisms. The jelly has been made using cresol red solution and slightly alkaline water. When it is placed in an acidic solution, the colour changes as the acid diffuses into the jelly and neutralises the alkali.

> **YOU WILL NEED**
>
> **Equipment:**
> • several transparent containers that can hold a cube with sides of 1 cm
> (e.g. boiling tubes or small beakers) • a ruler to measure in mm • a timer
> (e.g. on a phone) • a sharp knife or scalpel • a white tile or other surface for
> cutting • forceps • 1.0 mol dm^{-3} hydrochloric acid • agar jelly containing an
> alkali and cresol red indicator
>
> **Access to:**
> • distilled water

Safety considerations

- Make sure you have read the Safety advice section at the beginning of this book
  and listen to any advice from your teacher before carrying out this investigation.

- Take care with the sharp blade when cutting the agar pieces.

Method

1   Prepare cubes of jelly with sides of 5, 10 and 15 mm. If possible, prepare several
    cubes of each size.

2   Complete Table 4.3 to show the surface area and volume of each size of cube.

Length of side / mm	Surface area / mm²	Volume / mm³	Surface area : volume
5			
10			
15			

Table 4.3: Results table.

3   Pour dilute hydrochloric acid into a transparent container. Place one of your
    cubes in the acid, so that it is fully covered, and note the time taken for the whole
    cube to change colour.

4   Repeat with the other cubes.

5   Record your results in Results section.

> **TIP**
>
> If you can, repeat
> Step 3 twice more
> with different cubes of
> the same size.

Results

TIP

The independent variable is surface area : volume ratio, so this goes in the first column of your table.

Analysis, conclusion and evaluation

a   Use your results to describe the effect of surface area : volume ratio on the time taken for the hydrochloric acid to diffuse to the centre of the cube.

....

....

....

....

b   Discuss the extent to which you think your results can be considered to relate to real living organisms.

....

....

....

....

....

....

Practical Investigation 4.4: The effect of temperature or concentration gradient on the rate of diffusion

In Practical Investigation 4.3, you used agar jelly to measure the time taken for a substance to diffuse into the centre of an agar cube.

You can now use this technique to investigate a different independent variable. You have a choice of two – perhaps your teacher will arrange for different groups to investigate different variables, so that you can compare your results. You are going to plan your own experiment.

YOU WILL NEED

Equipment:

• several transparent containers that can hold a cube with sides of 1 cm (e.g. boiling tubes or small beakers) • a ruler to measure in mm • a timer (e.g. on a phone) • a sharp knife or scalpel • a white tile or other surface for cutting • forceps • about 250 cm³ 1.0 mol dm⁻³ hydrochloric acid • agar jelly containing an alkali and cresol red indicator • if you are investigating concentration gradient, you will also need several beakers, syringes or pipettes • if you are investigating temperature, you will also need several water baths set at different temperatures

Access to:

• distilled water

Safety considerations

• Make sure you have read the Safety advice section at the beginning of this book and listen to any advice from your teacher before carrying out this investigation.

• Take care with the sharp blade when cutting the agar pieces.

Method

1 Decide on your independent variable. It could be temperature, or it could be concentration of hydrochloric acid.

Independent variable to be investigated ....

2 Decide on the range and interval of your independent variable. Write down the values of the independent variable that you will use.

....

....

TIP

Remember that the range is the smallest and largest value for the independent variable. The interval is the 'gap' between each value. You should try to have at least five values.

3   What is your dependent variable?

....

4   How and when will you measure your dependent variable?

....

....

....

5   What variables will you need to standardise in your experiment? For each one, describe how you will keep it constant.

....

....

....

....

6   Will you use replicates in your experiment? If so, how many?

....

....

TIP

Be realistic about replicates. It is always good to do several replicates, but you will only have a limited amount of time.

7   Outline how you will do your experiment.

....

....

....

....

....

....

....

....

....

....

8   Carry out your experiment and record your results in a table in the space below.

You may decide to make changes to your plan as you work – this is often a very positive thing to do. Make a note of any changes that you made, and why.

....

....

....

....

....

Results

Analysis, conclusion and evaluation

a   Draw a line graph to display your results.

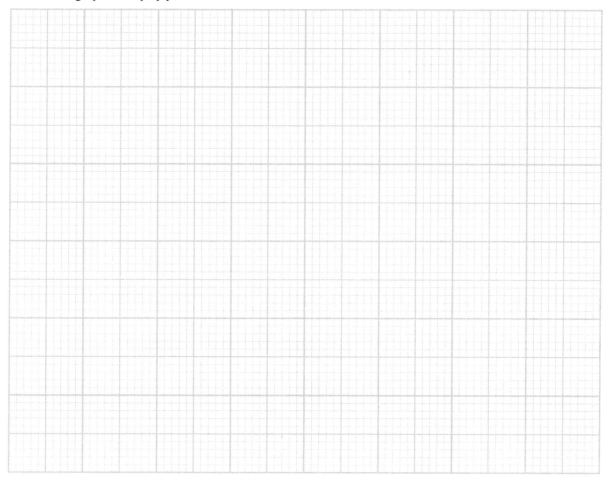

b   Use your results to describe the effect of your independent variable on the
dependent variable.

....

....

....

....

....

c List **three** significant sources of error that reduce the reliability of your results.

For each source of error, state whether this is a systematic or random error, and how it would affect your results.

source of error 1

....

....

source of error 2

....

....

source of error 3

....

....

Practical Investigation 4.5: Estimating the water potential of potato tuber cells

Potato tuber tissue is made up of many cells packed closely together. We can place pieces of potato tuber into solutions with different water potentials. If the water potential of the bathing solution is greater than that of the cell contents, then water will move into the cells by osmosis. The cells, and therefore the piece of potato tuber, will expand. However, if the water potential of the bathing solutions is less than that of the cell contents, then water will leave the potato cells by osmosis, and they will shrink.

If we can find the water potential of a bathing solution where the potato cells neither gain or lose water, then we know this is equal to the water potential of the cell contents.

YOU WILL NEED

Equipment:
- a large potato • a cork borer *or* a sharp knife or scalpel • seven containers, for example beakers, in which the potato cylinders can lie flat • a white tile or other surface for cutting • forceps • paper towel • about 50 cm^3 of six different concentrations of sucrose solution, ranging from 0.1 to 1 mol dm^{-3}
- a ruler to measure in mm and/or an electronic balance

Access to:
- distilled water

Safety considerations

- Make sure you have read the Safety advice section at the beginning of this book and listen to any advice from your teacher before carrying out this investigation.

- Take care with the cork borer or sharp blade when cutting the potato cylinders.

Method

You can either measure the change in length of the pieces of potato tuber, or you can measure the change in mass.

Decide which of these two measurements you will use, and write it here:

....

1   Peel the potato. Use the cork borer to cut seven cylinders of potato tuber, each with the same diameter. Cut each piece to the same length. Use the maximum length that you can, which will depend on the size of the potato.

2   Measure the mass *or* length of each cylinder, and place into a beaker. Record your initial measurements in Table 4.4.

3   Pour enough of the six sucrose solutions into the beakers to completely cover six of the potato cylinders. Pour water over the seventh cylinder. Leave for at least 30 min.

4   Remove each potato cylinder from the solution. Dry, then measure and record the final length or mass.

5   Calculate the percentage change in mass or length. Take care to state whether this is positive (an increase) or negative (a decrease).

> **TIP**
>
> As the masses and lengths are likely to vary slightly, make sure you know which piece has been placed in which beaker.

Results

Concentration of sucrose solution / mol dm⁻³	Initial .... of cylinder /	Final .... of cylinder /	Percentage change in ....

Table 4.4: Results table.

Analysis, conclusion and evaluation

a Draw a line graph to display your results.

b Use your graph to determine the concentration of sucrose solution in which the percentage change in length or mass of the potato pieces would be 0.

c The graph in Figure 4.2 shows the relationship between the concentration of a sucrose solution and its water potential.

Figure 4.2: Relationship between concentration of sucrose solution and its water potential.

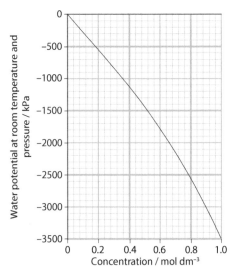

Use the graph, and your answer to **b**, to estimate the water potential of the contents of the potato cells.

....

d Discuss the degree of confidence that you have in the answer you have given to **c**.

....

....

....

....

....

....

e Suggest why measuring change in mass may be more likely to give a true value for water potential of the onion cells than measuring change in length.

....

....

....

....

Practical Investigation 4.6: Investigating plasmolysis in onion epidermis cells

In Practical Investigation 4.5, you investigated the effect of osmosis on whole tissues. In this investigation, you will study the effects of osmosis on individual cells within a tissue.

YOU WILL NEED

Equipment:

• an onion • a sharp knife or scalpel • several clean glass slides • several cover slips • a white tile or other surface for cutting • forceps • a seeker or mounted needle • a dropper pipette • filter paper or paper towel (for cleaning your slides) • a microscope and light source • about 50 cm³ of 1 mol dm⁻³ sucrose solution • syringes or pipettes to measure between 1 cm³ and 10 cm³

Access to:

• distilled water

Safety considerations

- Make sure you have read the Safety advice section at the beginning of this book and listen to any advice from your teacher before carrying out this investigation.

- Take care with the sharp blade when cutting the pieces of epidermis.

Method

1 You are provided with a $1 \, mol \, dm^{-3}$ sucrose solution. Use it to make up $10 \, cm^3$ of each of the following sucrose solutions: 0.3, 0.4, 0.5, 0.6, 0.7, 0.8 and $0.9 \, mol \, dm^{-3}$.

Use the space here to show how you will do this.

2 Put a drop of your first solution onto a clean microscope slide. Prepare a piece of onion epidermis approximately 6 mm square. (The exact dimensions are not important.) Put the onion epidermis into the drop of solution, and add more solution if necessary so that the epidermis is fully covered. Place a cover slip over the slide and leave for 2 or 3 min.

3 Observe your slide through the microscope. Using an appropriate objective lens, select a field of view where you can see a number of cells, and can distinguish whether or not they are plasmolysed. Count the total number of cells in your field of view, and the number that are plasmolysed. Move the slide and make another count. Repeat until you have counted at least 50 cells. Record your results in Table 4.5.

4 Repeat Steps 2 and 3 for each sucrose solution.

> **TIP**
>
> See Part 1 of Practical Investigation 1.1 for advice on how to make a temporary mount of onion epidermis.

Results

Concentration of sucrose solution / mol dm^{-3}	Total number of cells counted	Number of cells that were plasmolysed	Percentage of cells that were plasmolysed
0.3			
0.4			
0.5			
0.6			
0.7			
0.8			
0.9			
1.0			

Table 4.5: Results table.

In the space below, draw and label **one** cell that is not plasmolysed, and **one** cell that is plasmolysed.

Analysis, conclusion and evaluation

a   Draw a line graph to display your results. Draw a best-fit curve.

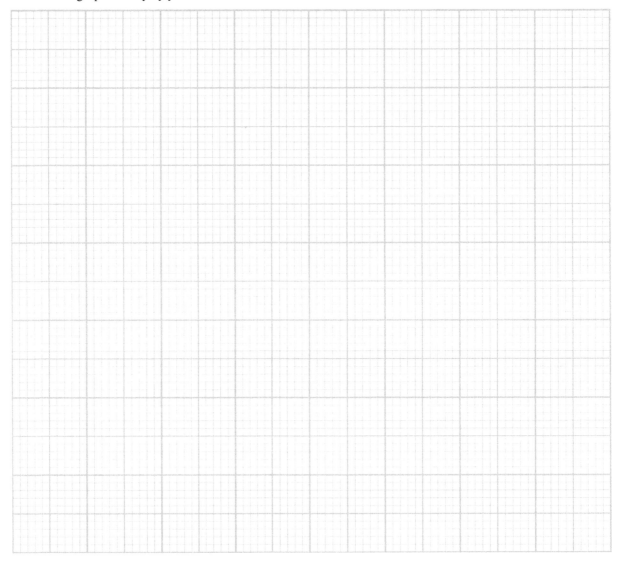

b   Explain the shape of the curve that you have drawn.

....

....

....

....

c   If you did this investigation again, using tisssue from a different onion, would you
    expect your results to be exactly the same? Explain your answer.

....

....

....

....

....

....

Practical Investigation 4.7: Determining water potential using density

Imagine you have a piece of plant tissue. You place it into a sucrose solution, and leave it long enough for osmosis to take place. Water will move into or out of the tissue until the water potential of the tissue and water potential of the sucrose solution are the same.

As this happens, the concentration of the sucrose solution changes. If the plant tissue originally had a higher water potential than the sucrose solution, then water will move *into* the sucrose solution and it will become *less* concentrated. If the plant tissue originally had a lower water potential than the sucrose solution, then water will move *out of* the sucrose solution into the plant tissue, and the sucrose solution will become *more* concentrated.

If we can find a sucrose solution that stays exactly the same concentration – it neither gains nor loses water – when we place our plant tissue into it, then this sucrose solution must have the same water potential as the plant tissue.

You are going to use density to determine this value.

*   You will make up a range of sucrose solutions. For each concentration, you will colour a sample of the sucrose solution blue.

*   You will cover plant tissue with the uncoloured solutions and leave them for long enough for osmosis to take place and the water potentials of the tissue and the sucrose solution to equalise.

*   Finally, you will place a drop of the blue version of the solution into the colourless sucrose solution of the same original concentration, which has had plant tissue in it. If the blue drop rises, this means the sucrose solution has become *more dense* – that is, it has lost water to the plant tissue. If the blue drop sinks, this means the sucrose solution has become *less dense* than it was originally – that is, it has gained water from the plant tissue.

Safety considerations

- Make sure you have read the Safety advice section at the beginning of this book and listen to any advice from your teacher before carrying out this investigation.

- Take care with the sharp blade when cutting the banana pieces.

Method

1 Place 5 cm³ of each concentration of sucrose solution into each of five labelled boiling tubes (see Figure 4.3). Place 5 cm³ of distilled water into the sixth tube.

2 Repeat Step 1 with a second set of labelled boiling tubes. For this second set, add a small drop of methylene blue solution to each solution. (This will make the solution look blue, but will not affect its water potential.)

3 Peel a banana and cut it in four lengthways. Cut one or two of the strips into 2 mm thick slices. You need 30 pieces altogether.

4 Place five pieces of banana into each of the *colourless* sucrose solutions and distilled water. Leave them for at least 10 min (or up to 30 min if you have time), to allow osmosis to take place.

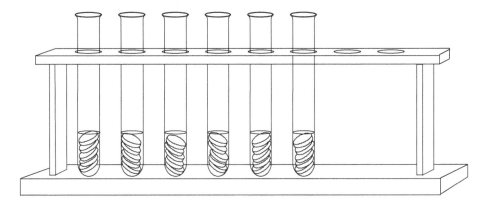

Figure 4.3: Apparatus for investigation 4.7.

5   While you are waiting, read through what you are going to do next, and make sure you understand it. Prepare a results table in the Results section.

6   Pour the sucrose solution from one of the tubes into a clean, labelled boiling tube. Using a dropper pipette, take a small quantity of the blue sucrose solution that was originally *of the same concentration*. Very gently place the tip of the pipette into the colourless sucrose solution, so that it is about 5 mm below the surface. Squeeze gently to introduce a drop of the blue sucrose solution into the colourless sucrose solution.

7   Watch the drop carefully, and note whether it rises, falls or remains in the same place.

8   Add another drop of coloured sucrose solution, and again note whether it rises, falls, or remains in the same place.

9   Now, slowly and carefully, repeat Steps 6, 7 and 8 for each of the other sucrose solutions.

Results

Analysis, conclusion and evaluation

a   Describe any pattern or trend that you can see in your results.

   ....

   ....

   ....

   ....

b Explain fully why some of the blue drops rose when placed into the sucrose solutions in which banana pieces had been soaking, and why some of them fell.

....

....

....

....

....

....

....

....

....

> **TIP**
>
> Use your own words for this answer – do not copy the explanation in the introduction to this investigation.

c Use your results to estimate the concentration of sucrose solution with the same water potential as the banana pieces.

....

d Discuss the degree of confidence that you have in your answer to **c**.

Your answer should include:

- the theory behind the design of the experiment, and whether you consider that this is a valid way to measure water potential
- significant sources of error that could affect how close your answer to **c** is to the 'true' value for the water potential of the banana pieces.

....

....

....

....

....

....

Practical Investigation 4.8: The effect of temperature on membrane permeability

Cell surface membranes are partially permeable – they allow some substances to pass through them, but not others. Beetroot cells contain a red pigment, called betalain, whose molecules are too large to pass through the cell surface membrane.

YOU WILL NEED

Equipment:
- beetroot cylinders, outer peel removed, that have been soaking in water
- sharp knife or scalpel • white tile or other surface for cutting • forceps
- several test tubes and a rack to hold them • a 250 cm^3 beaker • waterproof marker to label the test tubes • syringe to measure 20 cm^3

Access to:
- distilled water
- water baths at a range of at least five different temperatures

Safety considerations

- Make sure you have read the Safety advice section at the beginning of this book and listen to any advice from your teacher before carrying out this investigation.

- Take care with the sharp blade when cutting the beetroot pieces.

Method

1 Collect four beetroot cylinders, which have been soaking in water for several hours. Check with your teacher how many different temperatures you will be able to investigate. Cut this number of pieces from the beetroot cylinders, each 20 mm long.

2 Place all the beetroot cylinders into a container, and cover them with distilled water at room temperature. Shake them gently, so that any red pigment on the outside of the beetroot is washed off. Pour off the water, and repeat until no more red pigment leaves the beetroot pieces. Leave the beetroot pieces in the water while you complete the next steps.

3 Label a set of test tubes with the temperatures you will be testing and your name.

4 Take one test tube to one of the water baths. Use a syringe to measure 20 cm^3 of water from that water bath, and place in the test tube. Place the test tube in the water bath. Check the temperature with a thermometer, and record it in a suitable results table in the Results section. Repeat for the other test tubes.

5 Start a timer, and place one of the washed beetroot pieces into each of the test tubes. Leave them for 25 min.

6 Take the beetroot pieces out of the test tubes. (You do not need the beetroot pieces any more, so you can throw them away now.)

TIP

The labelling must be waterproof, as the tubes are going to be covered with water.

7   Place the test tubes in a rack, with a piece of white paper behind them. Decide on a simple way to describe the depth of colour in each tube. Record the colour in your results table.

Results

> **TIP**
>
> If you have access to a colorimeter, you can measure the absorbance of green light by the liquid in each tube, so that you will have a set of quantitative results.

Analysis, conclusion and evaluation

a   Describe any relationship that you can see between the depth of colour and the temperature.

....

....

....

b   Explain why the water in some of the tubes became coloured.

....

....

....

c   Explain the relationship between temperature and depth of colour that you have described in your answer to **a** above. You should refer to the structure of the cell surface membrane, and the effect of temperature on the kinetic energy of molecules.

....

....

....

....

....

....

d   Explain why each of the following steps was carried out:

   •   washing the beetroot pieces before placing in the water baths

   ....

   ....

   ....

   •   filling the test tubes with water from the water bath into which they were placed.

   ....

   ....

   ....

e   Compare your results with others in the class. Suggest reasons for any differences between the results from different groups.

....

....

....

....

....

f Suggest **two** ways in which this experiment could be improved. Explain each of your suggestions.

....

....

....

....

....

....

g Liquid X can affect the permeability of cell surface membranes. Outline how you could adapt this experiment to investigate the effect of different concentrations of Liquid X on the permeability of beetroot cell surface membranes.

....

....

....

....

....

....

....

....

....

....

> **TIP**
>
> Make sure that your answer clearly states your independent variable, the range and interval that you will use for your independent variable, how you will measure your dependent variable, and how you will standardise other significant variables.

> Chapter 5
Cell division and nucleic acids

Practical Investigation 5.1: Making a root tip squash

Introduction

In plants, cell division takes place only in certain parts of the plant. These are called **meristems**. There is a meristem just behind the root tip (Figure 5.1).

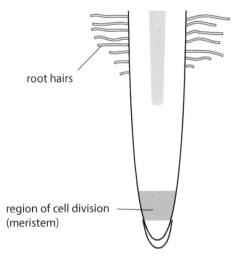

Figure 5.1: Line drawing of a root tip.

root hairs

region of cell division (meristem)

In this practical you will use young, actively-growing roots to **stain** and observe the chromosomes inside cells at different stages of the mitotic cell cycle.

The method of this practical is not difficult, but it *is* difficult to ensure success. If you cannot see dividing cells after your first attempt, have a look at Table 5.1 for suggestions.

YOU WILL NEED

Equipment:

• a young seedling (e.g. fava bean) or garlic clove with roots, or as supplied by your teacher • a clean microscope slide and a coverslip • a sharp knife, scalpel or safety razor blade • a means of heating the slide (Bunsen burner, spirit burner or hot plate) • mounted needle • filter paper • a small bottle of $1\,mol\,dm^{-3}$ hydrochloric acid, with a dropper • a small bottle of orcein ethanoic stain (acetic orcein stain), with a dropper • a watch glass or other small glass container • a white tile

Access to:

• distilled water

Safety considerations

• Make sure you have read the Safety advice section at the beginning of this book and listen to any advice from your teacher before carrying out this investigation.

• Avoid getting hydrochloric acid or orcein ethanoic stain onto your clothing or skin. If you do, wash immediately with cold water.

• Wear safety glasses throughout this practical.

• Take care when heating the watch glass in a flame, or on a hot plate.

Method

1 Place the seedling or garlic clove on the white tile. Cut neatly across a root about 1 cm back from the tip (Figure 5.2).

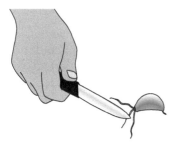

Figure 5.2: Method to cut off a root tip section.

---

2 Using a dropper pipette, place about 20 drops of orcein ethanoic stain and two drops of hydrochloric acid into a watch glass. You want enough stain to cover the root tip, so if this does not look enough, add more, keeping the proportions of stain and acid in the approximate ratio of 10 : 1.

Transfer the root tip to the stain, making sure that it is fully covered.

3 You now need to gently warm the root tip in the stain. This is quite tricky. If you do not warm it enough, the stain will not get into the cells and stain the chromosomes. If you warm it too much, you will damage the cells and chromosomes so much that you will not be able to see them when you look at the slide through a microscope.

Try one of these methods:

- Hold the watch glass in your fingers, and pass it forwards and backwards through a low Bunsen flame. If you hold it in your hand, this will stop you from letting it get too hot.

- Place the watch glass on a hot plate, and leave for about 5 min. Watch carefully to make sure that it does not look as though it is getting very hot.

4 Now remove the stained root tip from the watch glass and place it on a microscope slide. Add a couple of drops of stain.

5 Use a mounted needle to gently break the root tip apart. The aim is to separate the cells slightly, but to keep them in their same relative positions.

6 Cover with a coverslip. Try to avoid air bubbles. You can add more stain if there is not enough liquid between the coverslip and the slide.

7 Wrap a piece of filter paper around the slide and coverslip, to act as 'padding'. Use the blunt end of a pencil to gently tap repeatedly on the filter paper, gradually squashing the root tip. You can unwrap the filter paper every now and then to check how this is progressing. Be patient – it is better to take a long time rather than rushing and breaking the coverslip, when you will need to start all over again.

8 Warm the slide gently again, as in Step 3, but for only a very short period of time (e.g. about 10 s on the hot plate, or just a few passes through the flame).

9 Observe the slide through a microscope using the lowest power objective lens, and find the part of the squashed root tip where you can see cells dividing. Move up to a higher power objective if you think you can see chromosomes.

If you cannot see chromosomes, decide which of the issues in Table 5.1 is most likely to be the cause of the problem, and act according to the suggestions.

> **TIP**
>
> The cells to look for here are square-shaped.

Problem	Possible cause	Worth trying
you cannot see any cells	• you may have damaged the root too much, for example by leaving it in the hydrochloric acid mixture for too long, or by squashing it so much that the cells have all been pushed out from beneath the coverslip	• start again, handling the root tip more gently and reducing the time in the acid mixture
there are a lot of air bubbles on the slide, making it difficult to see the cells	• you trapped air bubbles underneath the coverslip when you lowered it	• remove the slide from the microscope stage • use a dropper pipette to gently add a small amount of stain at one edge of the coverslip, and allow it to run underneath • clean the slide before replacing it on the microscope stage
the cells are all piled up on top of one another, so you cannot see anything clearly	• you have not squashed the root tip enough	• remove the slide from the microscope stage • add more liquid if necessary, then wrap in filter paper and tap a little more strongly and for longer than you did before
you can see cells, but cannot make out any chromosomes	• the root cells may not have been dividing, so the chromosomes are not in their condensed state	• ask if other people in your class can see cells • if they can, try another root tip • if no-one can, you may need to try again at a different time of day (in some plants, mitosis takes place at particular times of day)
	• the chromosomes may not have taken up enough stain to become visible	• remove the slide from the microscope stage • remove the coverslip • add more stain and leave for a further 2 min • replace the coverslip and observe again under the microscope • if this does not work, start all over again, allowing longer in the stain
	• the slide may be over-stained	• start again, using a more dilute solution of the stain

Table 5.1: Troubleshooting guide.

Results

Try to identify cells in prophase, metaphase, anaphase and telophase. Anaphase is often the easiest to distinguish. The chromosomes look like tangled spider legs. Once you have identified a cell in anaphase, you may find it easier to identify other stages.

Make a labelled drawing of one cell in each stage that you can identify.

Note: if you are not able to identify these stages from your slide, return to this when you do Practical Investigation 5.2, and draw the stages using the prepared slide.

Practical Investigation 5.2: Investigating mitosis using prepared slides

Introduction

You may have been lucky (and careful!) in Practical Investigation 5.1, and succeeded in producing a superb slide with many visible dividing cells. However, this does not always happen, so in this investigation you will use a prepared slide to observe and analyse the different stages of the mitotic cell cycle.

YOU WILL NEED

Equipment:

• a microscope • a prepared slide of a root tip, stained to show cells undergoing mitosis

---

Safety considerations

- Make sure you have read the Safety advice section at the beginning of this book and listen to any advice from your teacher before carrying out this investigation.

- There are no significant safety issues associated with this practical investigation.

Method

1   Observe a prepared slide of a root tip under the microscope. Move the slide around until you can see cells with visible chromosomes.

2   Select an objective lens that allows you to see many cells in one field of view, and also to identify the stages of mitosis in the cells.

3   Select a field of view. Count the number of cells in each stage and enter tally marks in Table 5.2.

4   Repeat for different fields of view, until you have counted at least 50 cells. The more you count, the more reliable your results will be.

5   Count up your tallies for each stage, and complete Table 5.2.

> **TIP**
>
> Make sure that you move the slide far enough each time, so that you are not counting the same cells again. You need to be organised in how you do this.

Results

Stage	Interphase	Prophase	Metaphase	Anaphase	Telophase
Tally					
Number					

Table 5.2: Tally table.

Analysis, conclusion and evaluation

a Which of the stages in Table 5.2 are stages in mitosis?

....

b Calculate the mitotic index for the root.

mitotic index = the ratio of the number of cells in stages of mitosis to the number of cells in interphase

c Use the results in the tally chart to calculate the percentage of cells in each stage of the mitotic cell cycle.

Show your working.

d The relative numbers of cells in each stage of the cycle gives us a good indication of the relative time spent in each stage. For example, if 80% of cells are in interphase, this suggests that this stage takes up about 80% of the time for one cell cycle.

Assume that the total cell cycle in this plant takes 9 h.

Use your answer to question **c** to estimate the length of time that a cell spends in each stage of the mitotic cycle.

Show your working.

e Display your answer to question **d** as a pie chart.

f   Compare your calculated lengths of time with those of others in your class.
    Suggest reasons for any differences.

    ....

    ....

    ....

    ....

    ....

    ....

g   Suggest *and* explain how you could improve your method to increase your
    confidence in your results and conclusions.

    ....

    ....

    ....

    ....

    ....

Chapter 6

Plant transport

CHAPTER OUTLINE

This chapter relates to Chapter 7: Plant transport, in the Coursebook.

In this chapter, you will complete practical investigations on:

- 6.1 Drawing low-power plan diagrams of prepared sections of stems and roots
- 6.2 Drawing high-power diagrams of cells and tissues
- 6.3 Estimating the rate of water loss through the stomata of a leaf
- 6.4 Using a potometer
- 6.5 Investigating the effect of one factor on the rate of transpiration
- 6.6 Drawing sections and identifying the tissues of a typical leaf and a xerophytic leaf

Practical Investigation 6.1: Drawing low-power plan diagrams of prepared sections of stems and roots

You need to be able to identify different plant tissues and draw **plan diagrams**. The aim of drawing plan diagrams is to show the extent of different tissue types and not to draw individual cells.

KEY WORD

plan diagrams: a low-power diagram of something that shows tissues but not individual cells

YOU WILL NEED

Equipment:
- light microscope • eyepiece graticule • prepared sections of TS stem, and TS root of a dicotyledonous plant • pencil, HB or 2H grade • eraser • pencil sharpener • ruler

Safety considerations

- Make sure you have read the Safety advice section at the beginning of this book and listen to any advice from your teacher before carrying out this investigation.
- Take care when using lamps and microscopes as the bulbs can become very hot.

Method

Part 1: TS stem

1   Set up your microscope as shown in Chapter 1 with the low-power objective lens (×10) in place and with the eyepiece graticule in place.

2   Place the TS stem onto the microscope stage and bring it into focus using the low-power objective lens (×10).

3   You can often get a sharper image by adjusting the light intensity of the microscope. Adjust the light and condenser lens until a sharp, detailed image is seen. You may need your teacher to help you with this.

4   Try to identify the following tissue types in a region of the stem (Figures 6.1 and 6.2 should help you here): epidermis, fibres, phloem, xylem, cortex, vascular bundle.

5   Read the drawing guidance in the Practical skills chapter at the start of the book. Figures 6.1 and 6.2 show how a low-power plan diagram should be drawn.

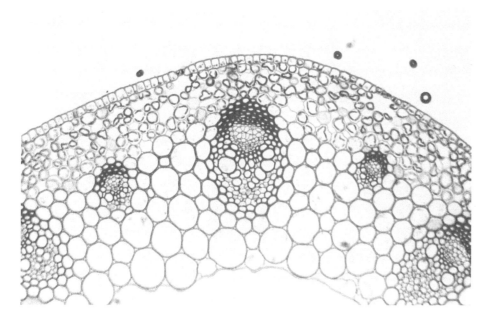

Figure 6.1: Photomicrograph of transverse section of stem.

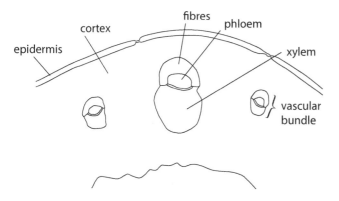

Figure 6.2: Low-power plan diagram of transverse section of stem.

6 Draw a low-power plan diagram of the TS stem in the space that follows, clearly labelling as many of the following as you can:

- epidermis
- fibres
- phloem
- xylem
- cortex
- vascular bundle

TIP
Do not redraw Figure 6.2!

Magnification: …………………..

7 The total magnification is the product of the eyepiece lens magnification (usually × 10) and the objective lens magnification (in this case × 10). So, for this diagram, the total magnification will be 10 × 10 = ×100. Include this information on your diagram.

8 Use the eyepiece graticule to count how many eyepiece units there are within the maximum length of a vascular bundle (from base of xylem to top of fibres) and record it in Table 6.1. Also, determine the maximum width of this vascular bundle and record it in Table 6.1.

9 Now record the maximum lengths and widths of four more vascular bundles and record them in Table 6.1.

Results

Vascular bundle	1	2	3	4	5	Mean
Length of vascular bundle / eyepiece units						
Width of vascular bundle / eyepiece units						

Table 6.1: Results table.

Analysis, conclusion and evaluation

Estimating the proportion of stem that is taken up by vascular bundle tissues

a Calculate the mean lengths and widths of the vascular bundles and record them in Table 6.1.

b Estimate and record the maximum diameter of the stem in eyepiece units (you may have to move the stem around if it is large). Count how many vascular bundles are present in the stem.

  i Number of vascular bundles: ....

  ii Maximum diameter of stem (eyepiece units):

    ....

c You can now estimate the proportion of stem that is made up of vascular bundle tissue. To do this you will have to calculate the cross-sectional areas of the vascular bundles and stem.

  i Total area of vascular bundles.

    Mean length of vascular bundles = ...

    Mean width of vascular bundles = ...

    If we assume that each vascular bundle is approximately an oval, we can calculate the area using the equation:

    $$\text{area} = \pi \times \left(\frac{\text{width}}{2}\right) \times \left(\frac{\text{length}}{2}\right)$$

    Mean estimated area of a vascular bundle = ...

    The total estimated area of vascular bundles = mean area × number of vascular bundles

    Total estimated area of vascular bundles = ...

  ii Cross-sectional area of stem.

    If we assume that the stem is a circle, the cross-sectional area can be calculated.

    Maximum diameter of stem: ....

    $$\text{area} = \pi \times \left(\frac{\text{diameter}}{2}\right)^2$$

    Total estimated area of stem = ...

iii   Proportional area.

The proportional area that is taken up by vascular bundles is:

Total estimated area of vascular bundles ÷ Total estimated area of stem

Proportional area of stem composed of vascular bundles = ...

Part 2: TS root

1   Take a prepared slide of TS root.

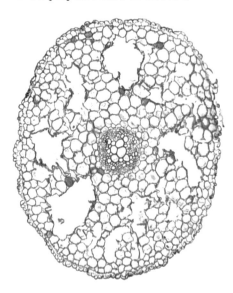

Figure 6.3: Photomicrograph of transverse section of root.

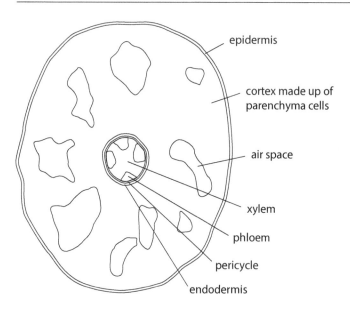

Figure 6.4: Low-power plan diagram of transverse section of root.

2   Draw a low-power plan diagram in the following space, again following the
    guidelines. Try to identify and label as many of the following structures as you can
    (Figures 6.3 and 6.4 should help you to identify them):

- epidermis

- cortex

- xylem

- phloem

- pericycle

- endodermis

Magnification: ....

3   Use the eyepiece graticule to estimate the maximum diameter of the stele (the
    central section of the root that contains xylem, phloem, pericycle and endodermis)
    and the maximum diameter of the whole root. Record these in the Results section.

Results

Diameter of stele: .... eyepiece units

Diameter of root: .... eyepiece units

Analysis, conclusion and evaluation

a You have determined the diameters of the stele and the root. Assuming that both structures are circular, calculate the areas of the stele and root.

> **TIP**
>
> area of circle =
> $\pi \times \left(\dfrac{\text{diameter}}{2}\right)^2$

Area of root: .... eyepiece units²

Area of stele: .... eyepiece units²

b Now, in the same way as with the stem, calculate the proportional area of the root that the stele covers. Show all your workings.

c Suggest reasons why your calculation of the proportion of the stem area that is composed of vascular tissue may not be accurate.

....

....

....

....

d Explain why units are not required for proportions of tissues.

....

....

....

....

Practical Investigation 6.2: Drawing high-power diagrams of cells and tissues

You need to be able to identify different cell and tissue types and draw high-power diagrams of cells. When drawing cells, you usually only need to draw a few (five or six) representative cells of each tissue type. Do not pick cells that have been damaged by the preparation of the section and try not to draw nuclei as solid shapes.

YOU WILL NEED

Equipment:
- microscope • eyepiece graticule • prepared sections of TS stem, TS leaf, TS root, LS stem, LS root • pencil, HB or 2H grade • eraser • pencil sharpener
- ruler

Safety considerations

- Make sure you have read the Safety advice section at the beginning of this book and listen to any advice from your teacher before carrying out this investigation.

- Take care when using lamps and microscopes as the bulbs can become very hot.

Method

Part 1: TS stem

1   Set up your microscope as you did in Chapter 1.

2   Examine a prepared section of TS stem using low power and find a vascular bundle.

3   Change to the high-power objective lens and look carefully at the vascular bundle.

4   Use the drawing guidance in the Practical skills chapter at the beginning of the book and draw five or six cells that are joined together of as many of these tissues as possible:

   - xylem

   - phloem (both sieve tube elements with attached companion cells)

   - epidermis

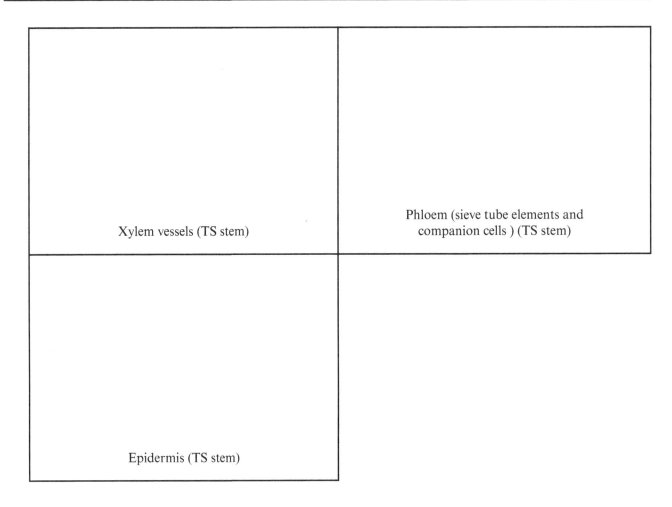

Xylem vessels (TS stem)	Phloem (sieve tube elements and companion cells) (TS stem)
Epidermis (TS stem)	

Use the eyepiece graticule to draw a scale bar with ten graduations on each diagram. This is to help you understand the proportions of the cells and tissues. You do not need to calibrate the graticule.

Part 2: TS root

1   Now, swap the slide for a slide with TS root. Identify the vascular tissue in the centre of the root using low power.

2   Change to the high-power objective lens and draw five or six cells that are joined together of:

- epidermis

- pericycle and endodermis (the pericycle is the layer just beneath the endodermis)

- parenchyma (cortex cells)

Epidermis (TS root)

Pericycle and endodermis (TS root)

Parenchyma (TS root)

Use the eyepiece graticule to draw a scale bar with ten graduations on each diagram. You do not need to calibrate the graticule.

Part 3: TS leaf

1   Now, swap the slide for a slide with TS leaf. Using the high-power objective lens, identify the main tissue types and draw five or six cells that are joined together of:

- palisade mesophyll

- spongy mesophyll

- lower epidermis (including guard cells)

- upper epidermis

- collenchyma (found in mid-rib)

Palisade mesophyll (TS leaf)	Spongy mesophyll (TS leaf)
Lower epidermis (TS leaf)	Upper epidermis (TS leaf)
Collenchyma (TS leaf)	

Use the eyepiece graticule to draw a scale bar with ten graduations on each diagram. You do not need to calibrate the graticule.

Part 4: LS stem and LS root

1 Finally, look at the slides of LS stem and LS root. These are sections that have been cut longitudinally so should give an idea of the lengths of different cells.

2 Try to find and draw clear examples (three of four cells) of:

- sieve tube elements with attached companion cells

- xylem vessels (it may be possible to see rings of lignin along the vessels)

<table>
<tr><td>Xylem vessels (LS stem or root)</td><td></td></tr>
<tr><td>Phloem (LS stem or root)</td><td>Other structures</td></tr>
</table>

Analysis, conclusion and evaluation

a   Use your drawings to compare and contrast the structures of the following pairs of cell types. Consider the sizes and the cells, shapes and other structures.

   i   xylem vessels and phloem (both TS and LS)

   ....

   ii   stem epidermis and root epidermis

   ....

   iii   lower and upper leaf epidermis

   ....

   iv   palisade mesophyll and spongy mesophyll

   ....

b   Xylem vessels are hollow, dead cell types that contain lignin in their cell walls. Lignin strengthens the cells and is impermeable to water. Explain why these cells are dead and how lignin is important to their function.

   ....

   ....

c   Explain how the following cell types and tissues are adapted for their functions.
    You will have to use some of your own knowledge here.

    i   phloem

    ....

    ....

    ii lower leaf epidermis

    ....

    ....

    iii root epidermis

    ....

    ....

    iv collenchyma cells

    ....

    ....

d   Explain why sections need to be one cell thick.

    ....

    ....

Practical Investigation 6.3: Estimating the rate of water loss through the stomata of a leaf

In this practical you will learn how to estimate the number of stomata present in the leaves of a plant and use a simple method for determining the rate of water loss.

Part 1: Measuring the water loss (Days 1–7)

> **YOU WILL NEED**
>
> **Equipment:**
> • a suitable branch of a plant with approximately ten leaves • a measuring cylinder, 100 cm³ • paraffin oil in a dropper bottle, 50 cm³ • a source of tap water

Safety considerations

• Make sure you have read the Safety advice section at the beginning of this book and listen to any advice from your teacher before carrying out this investigation.

• Take care that you have no allergy problems with the plant species used.

Method

1 Take a small branch of a plant and remove most of the lower leaves so that a long branch is left with about ten leaves at the end of it.

2 Cut the lower end of the branch and place it into a 100 cm³ measuring cylinder.

3 Fill the measuring cylinder up to 100 cm³ with water.

4 Carefully pour a layer of paraffin oil over the surface of the water (see Figure 6.5).

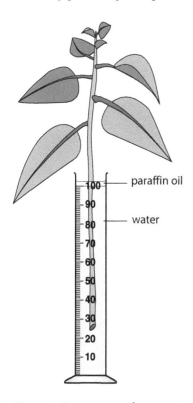

Figure 6.5: Apparatus for investigation 6.3.

5   Leave the measuring cylinder and plant in a well-lit, ventilated area for seven days.

6   After seven days, measure the volume of water (underneath the paraffin oil). Record this in the Results section.

Results

Volume of water in measuring cylinder after seven days:......................................

Analysis, conclusion and evaluation

a   i   Calculate the mean rate of water loss per day using these instructions:

water lost after seven days = $100\,cm^3$ – volume of water left in measuring cylinder

mean loss of water per day = volume of water lost after 7 days ÷ time taken

The experiment was carried out for seven days. Use the equations to calculate the mean loss of water per day.

Mean loss of water per day = ...$cm^3\,day^{-1}$

   ii   Now, convert this value to mean loss of water per hour by dividing it by 24.

Mean loss of water per hour = ...$cm^3\,h^{-1}$

   iii   Now, convert the units to $mm^3\,h^{-1}$ by multiplying by 1000.

Mean loss of water per hour = ... $mm^3\,h^{-1}$

Part 2: Estimating the leaf surface area (Day 7)

YOU WILL NEED

Equipment:
- a selection of grid paper for tracing around the leaves, for example 10, 5, 2 and 1 mm. If they are not available, graph paper will work.

Safety considerations

- As for Part 1.

Method

1   Remove the branch from the measuring cylinder and give each leaf a number. Use a random number generator to select five random numbers.

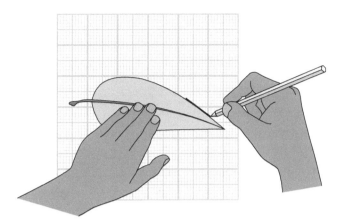

Figure 6.6: Method for part 2 of investigation 6.3: tracing around a leaf.

2   Remove the leaves that have been selected and trace around each leaf with a pencil onto a piece of grid paper (shown in Figure 6.6). The spacing on the grid paper can be 2, 1.5, 1.0 or 0.5 cm. Depending on the sizes of the leaves, you should choose a grid size that will give accurate results but not take too long to count all the squares.

3   To calculate the surface area of the leaves, count the number of squares that each leaf covers. For squares that are only partly covered by the leaf outline, count all these partially filled squares and divide the total by two. Record the results in Table 6.2 below.

Results

	Leaf number				
	1	2	3	4	5
Number of whole squares					
Number of part squares					
Number of part squares ÷ 2					
Total number of squares					

Table 6.2: Results table.

Total number of leaves on branch: ....

Analysis, conclusion and evaluation

a   i   Calculate the mean surface area of the leaves by adding together the total number of squares for all five leaves and dividing by five.

mean leaf surface area = total number of squares for each leaf ÷ 5

Mean leaf surface area = ... squares

ii   To convert number of squares into metric units, you must calculate the area of one square. This will depend on the grid size you used.

Area of one square = ... mm²

iii Calculate the mean leaf surface area using the following formula:

mean leaf surface area = 2 × (mean number of squares × area of one square)

Mean leaf surface area = ... mm²

iv   You can now calculate the total leaf surface area of all the leaves on your branch using the following formula:

total leaf surface area = (number of leaves × mean leaf surface area)

Total leaf surface area = ... mm²

v   The total leaf surface area is the combined surface areas of upper and lower epidermis. If we want to find the surface area of the upper and lower epidermis we simply divide the total leaf surface area by two.

Surface area of upper epidermis = ... mm²

Surface area of lower epidermis = ... mm²

Part 3: Estimating total number of stomata (Day 7)

YOU WILL NEED

Equipment:

• clear (transparent) nail varnish • forceps • mounted needle • microscope slides • coverslips • light microscope • stage micrometer

Safety considerations

•   As for Part 1.

•   Eye protection should be used when using nail varnish.

Method

1   Paint a leaf with clear nail varnish on the top and bottom sides. Leave it to dry.

2   When fully dry, use a pair of forceps to carefully peel the nail varnish from the lower side of the leaf (see Figure 6.7).

3   Place the nail varnish peel onto a microscope slide in a drop of water, and place a coverslip over the top.

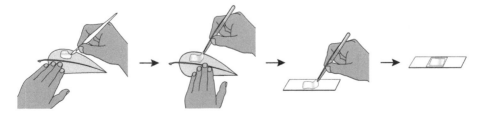

Figure 6.7: Method for part 3 of investigation 6.3: making stomatal peels.

4   Set up a microscope with an eyepiece graticule in place as you did in Chapter 1.

5   View the nail varnish peel using the high-power objective lens and locate the stomata.

6   Count the number of stomata in the field of view.

7   Count the stomata in four more areas of the leaf and record your results in Table 6.3.

8   Repeat this for the upper epidermis nail varnish peel, again recording your results in Table 6.3.

9   With the same objective lens in place, use a stage micrometer to calibrate the eyepiece graticule. Now, use the eyepiece graticule to estimate the diameter of the field of view and record this below Table 6.3.

> **TIP**
>
> If unsure how to do this, check back to Chapter 1.

Results

Field of view number	Number of stomata in field of view	
	lower epidermis	upper epidermis
1		
2		
3		
4		
5		
mean		

Table 6.3: Results table

Diameter of field of view = ... µm

Convert this value to mm by diving by 1000.

Diameter of field of view = ... mm

Analysis, conclusion and evaluation

a   i   Calculate the area of one field of view by using the formula:

$$\text{area} = \pi \times \left(\frac{\text{diameter}}{2}\right)^2$$

Area of one field of view = ... mm²

ii Calculate the mean number of stomata per field of view:

Mean number of stomata in lower epidermis = ... stomata per field of view

Mean number of stomata in upper epidermis = ... stomata per field of view

iii You can now calculate the mean number of stomata on the lower and upper epidermis by dividing the mean number of stomata per field of view by the area of the field of view.

Mean number of stomata per square millimetre in lower epidermis = ... mm^{-2}

Mean number of stomata per square millimetre in lower epidermis = ... mm^{-2}

iv Now that you know the surface areas of the lower and upper epidermis and the mean numbers of stomata per square millimetre, you can calculate the total number of stomata.

total number of stomata on lower epidermis = surface area of lower epidermis × mean number of stomata on lower epidermis per square millimetre

total number of stomata on upper epidermis = surface area of lower epidermis × mean number of stomata on lower epidermis per square millimetre

The total number of stomata on lower epidermis = ...

The total number of stomata on upper epidermis = ...

To calculate the total number of stomata on the branch, you can now add together the number of stomata on lower and upper epidermis.

Total number of stomata = ...

v You should now have calculated:

- the mean rate of water loss in $mm^3 h^{-1}$ from the branch

- the total number of stomata.

We can now use these data to calculate the mean rate of water loss per stomata.

mean rate of water loss = rate of water loss ÷ total number of stomata

Mean rate of water loss per stomata = ... $mm^3 h^{-1}$ $stomata^{-1}$

b Explain why five leaves were selected at random.

....

....

c Explain how it would affect **i** the estimation of the total leaf surface area, and **ii** the estimated rate of water loss per stomata, if all the leaves selected were smaller than the mean size.

i total leaf surface area

....

....

ii estimated rate of water loss per stomata.

....

....

d Explain why paraffin oil was placed over the water.

....

....

e The mean rate of water loss was estimated over a seven-day period. Explain four factors that could have caused differences in the rate of water loss.

1 ....

....

2 ....

....

3 ....

....

4 ....

....

f Suggest three sources of inaccuracy in the experiment and in each case suggest an improvement.

1 inaccuracy ....

....

improvement ....

....

2   inaccuracy ....

....

    improvement ....

....

3   inaccuracy ....

....

    improvement ....

....

Practical Investigation 6.4:
Using a potometer

A potometer is a piece of equipment that measures the water loss from a plant. In this investigation, you will learn how to set up a volume potometer to measure the rate of water loss, *transpiration*, from a branch. We actually measure the rate water is taken up by a shoot and make the assumption that all the water that is taken up is lost by the leaves.

YOU WILL NEED

Equipment:
- a branch with several leaves attached • a potometer (see Figure 6.8)
- beaker, 250 cm³ • ruler, graduated in millimetres • secateurs (to cut the branch) • filter paper • timer • retort stand, two clamps and two bosses
- piece of stiff card, A4 size • glass marker pen

Access to:
- deep sink or water trough • tap water

Safety considerations

- Make sure you have read the Safety advice section at the beginning of this book and listen to any advice from your teacher before carrying out this investigation.

- Take care that you have no allergy problems with the plant species used.

- Take care cutting with the secateurs and with glass potometers which can break and cause cuts.

- Eye protection should be worn when using the capillary tubing and putting equipment together.

Method

1 Fill up the sink or trough with tap water.

2 Take a branch with several leaves attached and place it under water.

3 Place the potometer underwater in the sink and fill it with water (check that there are no air bubbles).

4 While holding the branch underwater, cut the lower end with the secateurs at an approximately 45° angle. Do not take it out of the water at any point as this will introduce bubbles into xylem vessels.

5 Carefully push the cut end of the stem into the rubber tubing of the potometer (see Figure 6.8), keeping all the equipment under water at all times.

Figure 6.8: Method for investigation 6.4: setting up a potometer.

6 Check there are no air bubbles in the rubber tube of the potometer (there should be a continuous column of water from the end of the stem into the glass capillary tubing).

7 Remove the potometer and branch from the water and clamp it upright as shown in Figure 6.9.

8 Carefully dry the surfaces of the leaves with tissue paper.

9 Touch the end of the glass capillary tubed with the filter paper to allow air to enter the end of the tube.

10 When some air has entered the base of the capillary tube, hold the 250 cm³ beaker of water so that the end of the capillary tube is in the water. Leave it for a minute or until some water has entered allowing an air bubble to form.

Mark where the air bubble is on the glass capillary tube with the glass marker pen.

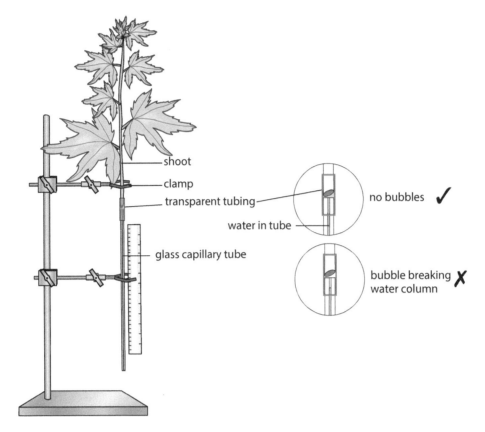

Figure 6.9: A potometer.

11 Leave the apparatus for 5 min and then mark the position where the bubble has moved to.

12 Repeat this for four more intervals of 5 min.

13 Using the ruler, measure the distance the bubble moved during each of the 5 min intervals. Record your results in Table 6.4.

14 Measure the radius of the capillary tube using the ruler.

Results

Time / min	Distance moved by air bubble / mm
5	
10	
15	
20	
25	

Table 6.4: Results table.

Radius of capillary tube: .... mm

TIP

If at any point air bubbles have broken the column of water in the rubber tube, the apparatus must be taken apart and put together again under water. If the air bubble in the capillary tube reaches the rubber tube, a new air bubble can be introduced by placing the end of the capillary tube in the beaker of water.

Analysis, conclusion and evaluation

a   Calculate the mean distance moved by the air bubble per 5 min interval.

  Mean distance moved per 5 min interval = ... mm

  Now, calculate the mean distance moved per minute by dividing this number by 5 min:

  Mean distance moved per minute = ... mm min^{-1}

b   To calculate the volume of water lost, we assume that the capillary tube is a cylinder and need to calculate its volume.

  where r is the radius and l is the length of the water (distance moved by the bubble).

  Volume of water lost per minute = ...

> **TIP**
>
> volume = $\pi \times r^2 \times l$

c   Explain why the calculated value of volume of water lost per minute may not necessarily be the actual volume of water lost from the leaves.

  ....

  ....

  ....

  ....

> **TIP**
>
> Do not forget to add your units!

d   Give **three** functions of transpiration.

  ....

  ....

  ....

  ....

e   Explain why it was important to ensure that no air enters the xylem.

  ....

  ....

  ....

  ....

f Explain why the leaves were dried.

....

....

....

....

g Describe the variation in water loss over each 5 min period of your experiment. State whether the values were similar. If not, suggest reasons for changes in the rate of water loss.

....

....

....

....

h Compare your rate of water loss with the results from other members of your class. Suggest reasons for any differences.

....

....

....

....

Practical Investigation 6.5: Investigating the effect of one factor on the rate of transpiration

In Practical Investigation 6.4, you learnt how to set up and use a potometer. In this planning investigation, you will plan and carry out an investigation, using a photometer, into the effect of a factor on the rate of transpiration of a plant.

Planning

Complete Table 6.5 to explain how different factors will affect transpiration rate and how you could change them in a practical. The first one has been done for you.

Factor affecting transpiration rate	Why it affects transpiration rate	How increasing it will affect transpiration rate	How you could change it in your practical
temperature	• affects kinetic energy of water molecules • affects speed of movement of water molecules • affects how saturated with water air is • affects evaporation of water	• increasing temperature increases rate of transpiration	• place plant at different distances from a heater, measuring the air temperature with a thermometer • use a heater with different settings • possible heat sources could be radiators / Bunsen burners
humidity			
wind speed			

Factor affecting transpiration rate	Why it affects transpiration rate	How increasing it will affect transpiration rate	How you could change it in your practical
light intensity			

Table 6.5: Results table.

Variables

1   You will need to plan the practical so that it produces valid data. Fill in the sections below to help you in your written plan. You need to calculate rate of transpiration so you will need to have a measure of both water loss and a time over which is has occurred.

a   i   The independent variable is: ....

   ii   The different values I will investigate are (choose five different values):

      ....

   iii   The number of replicates of each value: ....

   iv   How I will change the independent variable:

      ....

      ....

   v   The dependent variable is: ....

   vi   I will measure this by:

      ....

      ....

2 To make the experiment valid, you will need to consider every other factor that will affect the rate of transpiration and how the steps you will take ensure that it does not change. These factors are the standardised variables. In some cases, it will not be easy to prevent changes but you should watch carefully to identify how much it did change.

Variable	How I will standardise the variable

Table 6.6: Results table.

YOU WILL NEED

List the equipment you will need:

- ....
- ....
- ....

- ....
- ....
- ....

Safety considerations

- Make sure you have read the Safety advice section at the beginning of this book.

- You will need to think about what risks your practical has and what can be done to reduce the risks. This could include precautions such as care when cutting stems, wearing eye protection or how to deal with spills of chemicals.

Risk	Reducing the risk

Table 6.7: Safety considerations.

Method

Now write a full written step-by-step plan as to what you intend to do. Give your investigation a title (e.g. An investigation into the effect of changing ....
on ....) and list any specific equipment you will need. Include all practical details, how you will change the independent variable, measure the dependent variable and standardise all other variables.

TIP

Have another look at Practical Investigation 6.4 to work out how to calculate the volume of water lost and how to calculate the rate of water loss.

....

....

....

....

....

....

....

....

....

....

....

....

....

....

....

....

....

....

The plan will need to be checked by your teacher before you go ahead and carry out the experiment.

Results

Record your results in Table 6.8 or draw your own if your experiment is slightly different.

Independent variable	Distance moved by bubble / mm				Volume of water lost / mm³	Time taken / min	Rate of water loss / mm³ min⁻¹
	1	2	3	mean			

Table 6.8: Results table.

Diameter of capillary tube: .... mm

Time taken for bubble to move: .... min

Analysis, conclusion and evaluation

You should have three sets of data for your chosen values of the independent variable.

a Calculate the mean distances moved by the bubbles and record these in Table 6.8.

b Use the following equation to calculate the volume of water lost and record your answers in the table.

volume of water lost = $\pi \times$ (diameter $\div$ 2)^2 $\times$ distance moved by bubble c   Record the time taken for the measurements in Table 6.8.

d   Calculate the mean rate of water loss in mm³ min⁻¹ and record this in Table 6.8.

e   Use the following grid to plot a graph of rate of water loss (*y*-axis) against your independent variable (*x*-axis).

f Describe the effect of increasing the independent variable on the rate of transpiration.

....

....

g Explain the effect of increasing the independent variable on the rate of transpiration.

....

....

....

....

h Explain why changing the independent variable creates difficulties with maintaining the standardised variables.

....

....

....

....

Practical Investigation 6.6: Drawing sections and identifying the tissues of a typical leaf and a xerophytic leaf

You need to be able to identify the different tissues in a leaf and understand the adaptations of xerophytic plants.

YOU WILL NEED

Equipment:
• light microscope • eyepiece graticule • prepared sections of TS leaf of a dicotyledonous plant and TS leaf of *Ammophila* • pencil, HB or 2H grade • eraser • pencil sharpener • ruler

Safety considerations

- Make sure you have read the Safety advice section at the beginning of this book and listen to any advice from your teacher before carrying out this investigation.

- Take care when using lamps and microscopes as the bulbs can become very hot.

Method

1 Take a prepared slide of TS leaf.

2 Bring an area into focus that has a section of mid-rib and leaf blade.

3 Draw a low-power plan diagram, again following the guidelines. Try to identify and label as many of the following structures as you can (Figures 6.10 and 6.11 should help you to identify them):

- cuticle
- upper epidermis
- lower epidermis (including stomata)
- palisade mesophyll
- spongy mesophyll
- xylem (this may be in found in the mid-rib and the leaf blade)
- phloem (this may be found in the mid-rib and the leaf blade)
- vascular bundle
- parenchyma (this tissue is made up of unspecialised cells)
- collenchyma (this tissue is made up of cells that are very similar to parenchyma cells but have thicker cell walls for extra support. It may be difficult to identify where parenchyma and collenchyma tissue start and end)

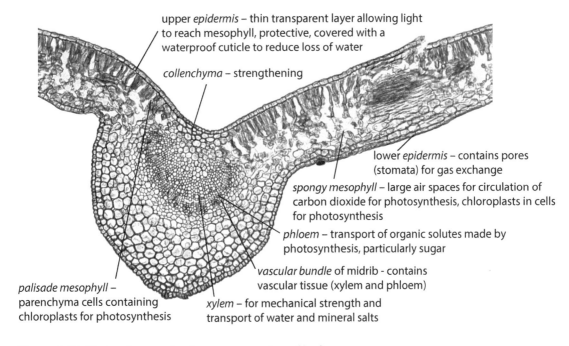

Figure 6.10: Photomicrograph of transverse section of leaf.

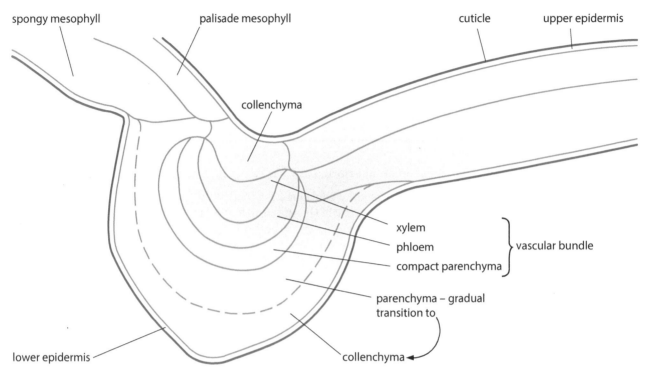

Figure 6.11: Low-power plan diagram of transverse section of leaf.

Magnification: ....

4 Now take the TS of *Ammophila*. This is a xerophyte that is able to grow in areas of very low water. Draw a tissue map of the leaf and try to identify the following tissues and structures:

- cuticle
- upper epidermis
- lower epidermis (including stomata)
- palisade mesophyll
- spongy mesophyll
- xylem (this may be in found in the mid-rib and the leaf blade)
- phloem (this may be found in the mid-rib and the leaf blade)
- vascular bundle
- pits in lower epidermis
- trichomes (hairs)

You should use Figure 6.12 to help you identify the structures but do not copy it out!

5   Add some notes to your diagram to explain how the leaf is adapted to reduce water loss. You should focus on:

-   rolling of the leaf

-   thickness of cuticle / epidermis

-   woodiness of leaf

-   presence of trichomes

-   stomatal pits

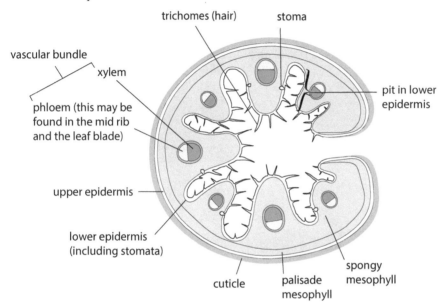

Figure 6.12: Low-power plan diagram of transverse section of *Ammophila*.

Analysis, conclusion and evaluation

a   Describe **four** differences between the structures of the typical dicotylendous leaf and *Ammophila*.

    ....

    ....

    ....

    ....

b   Explain how the structure of the *Ammophila* leaf enables the plant to survive in
    low water areas.

    ....

    ....

    ....

    ....

Chapter 7

Mammalian transport and gas exchange

This chapter relates to Chapter 8: Transport in mammals and Chapter 9: Gas exchange, in the Coursebook.

In this chapter, you will complete practical investigations on:

- 7.1 Identifying and drawing blood cells

- 7.2 Observing and drawing the structures of the heart

- 7.3 Observing and drawing the different structures of arteries, veins and capillaries

- 7.4 Observing and drawing the structure of the respiratory system and its tissues

Practical Investigation 7.1: Identifying and drawing blood cells

Blood has four main components: plasma, erythrocytes (red blood cells), leukocytes (white blood cells) and thrombocytes (platelets). There are many different types of leukocytes, including monocytes, neutrophils and lymphocytes. You need to be able to identify these different cells.

YOU WILL NEED

Equipment:
- light microscope • prepared section of blood • pencil, HB or 2H grade
- eraser • pencil sharpener • ruler

Safety considerations

- Make sure you have read the Safety advice section at the beginning of the book and listen to any advice from your teacher before carrying out this investigation.

Method

1 Set up your microscope as shown in Chapter 1.

2 Place the blood slide on the stage using the low-power objective lens and bring some of the cells into focus.

3   Change to a higher-power objective lens and use the fine focus to bring the individual blood cells into focus.

4   Spend some time moving the slide around carefully in order to try to identify the different blood cell types. Use Figure 7.1, a photomicrograph of human blood cells, to help you to identify:

- erythrocytes
- monocytes
- lymphocytes
- neutrophils

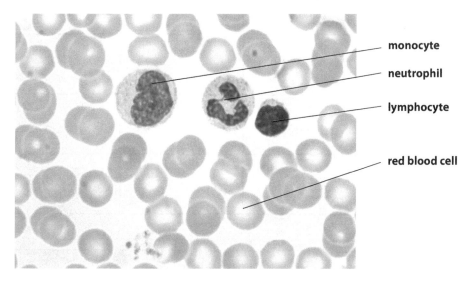

Figure 7.1: Photomicrograph of blood cells.

KEY WORDS

red blood cells: these are the largest number of cells and appear spherical with a paler centre

monocytes (white blood cells): these are large cells with a nucleus that is large and often kidney-shaped

lymphocytes (white blood cells): these are smaller, spherical cells with a large circular nucleus that takes up a large proportion of the cell

neutrophils (white blood cells): these are large cells with a lobed nucleus

5   Using the drawing rules described in the Practical skills chapter at the start of the book, draw two or three cells of each type in the Results section. Add notes to help with your descriptions.

Results

Erythrocytes	Monocytes
Lymphocytes	Neutrophils

TIP

Do not forget to add labels and record the magnification. Remember, you should be able to distinguish between different cell types.

Analysis, conclusion and evaluation

a   Complete Table 7.1 to compare the structures of the four types of blood cell.

Cell type	Nucleus present (y / n)	Shape of nucleus	Colour	Other distinguishing features
erythrocyte				
monocyte				
lymphocyte				
neutrophil				

Table 7.1: Comparison of structures.

b   Complete Table 7.2 to match the names of each of the blood cells to its function.

Name of blood cell	Function
	• transported around body in blood and ingest pathogens by phagocytosis
	• exist in two major groups, T-cells and B-cells • involved in the immune response including production of antibodies
	• contain haemoglobin and transport oxygen around the body
	• transported around the blood eventually settling in organs to mature as macrophages which ingest pathogens by phagocytosis

Table 7.2: Blood cell functions.

c   Figures 7.2–7.4 are photomicrographs of blood cells taken from a normal patient (Figure 7.2), a patient with leukaemia (a bone marrow cancer) (Figure 7.3), and a patient with sickle cell anaemia (Figure 7.4).

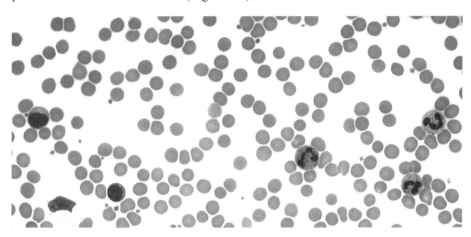

Figure 7.2: Photomicrograph of normal blood cells.

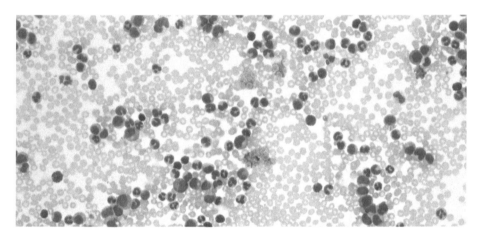

Figure 7.3: Photomicrograph of blood cells from a patient with leukaemia.

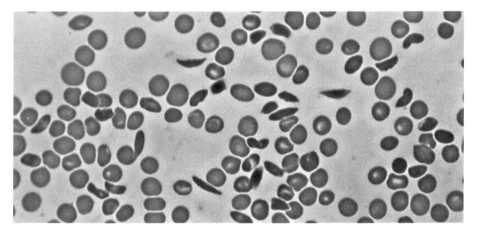

Figure 7.4: Photomicrograph of blood cells from a patient with sickle cell anaemia.

Describe how the blood from the patients with leukaemia and sickle cell anaemia differs from the normal blood. Suggest some symptoms that these patients may have due to their blood (you may wish to do some independent research here).

i   Leukaemia patient
Differences:

....

....

Possible symptoms and effects:

....

....

ii   Sickle cell anaemia patient
Differences:

....

....

Possible symptoms and effects:

....

....

Practical Investigation 7.2: Observing and drawing the structures of the heart

Dissection is an important skill in the study of biology. The aim is to observe the anatomical features of organs and be able to relate them to their functions. It is important to take your time to appreciate the design of the organs and not rush to cut things open. Drawings, or possibly photographs, should be taken at repeated periods of time when key structures are exposed.

The heart is an easy organ to dissect as it is easy to see the functional architecture of structures such as the chambers, valves and blood vessels.

> **YOU WILL NEED**
>
> **Equipment:**
> - scalpels • dissection scissors • mounted needle • forceps • tray
> - heart (sheep)
>
> **Access to:**
> - sink • running water • hand-washing facilities • gloves if requested
> - sterilising fluid and cloths

Safety considerations

- Make sure you have read the Safety advice section at the beginning of this book and listen to any advice from your teacher before carrying out this investigation.

- Eye protection should be worn.

- Dissection equipment is sharp so caution should be taken. When using scalpels, keep fingers well away from the blade and only apply light pressure.

- Wash hands with soap and warm water afterwards. Gloves may be worn if required.

- After completing the dissection, all work surfaces should be washed with disinfectant and dissection equipment placed into disinfectant.

Method

1   Take the heart and lay it in the tray. Examine the shape of and location of the blood vessels. The quality of hearts obtained for dissection may vary and sometimes some of the structures, such as the arteries and atria, may have been removed. The arteries at the top of the heart have thick, white walls. The veins are more difficult to identify and have often been removed but there will be holes at the tops of the left and right atria where they would enter the heart. Look inside the arteries and see if you can identify the semilunar valves at their bases.

2   Locate the atria on both sides of the heart (see Figure 7.5) and then use your fingers to feel the ventricles that the atria lead to. You should be able to identify the left and right ventricles by inserting your index finger into each ventricle and feeling the thickness of the walls. The side with a thinner wall will be the right ventricle.

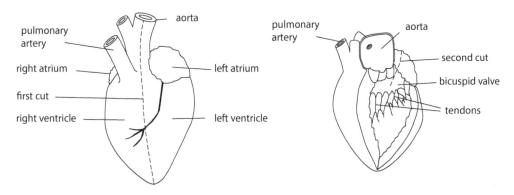

Figure 7.5: Drawing of external and internal structures of a heart.

3   Identify the coronary blood vessels that run across the front of the heart (see Figure 7.5) and lay the heart in the tray as shown in Figure 7.5. Try to locate:

- coronary blood vessels
- aorta
- pulmonary artery
- left and right atria
- left and right ventricles

4   Take a scalpel or scissors and cut from the top of the aorta down to the apex of the heart as shown in Figure 7.5. It should now be possible to open out the ventricle and observe the semilunar valve at the base of the aorta, bicuspid valve between the ventricle and atrium, and the thickness of the ventricle wall.

5   Now, cut upward into the left atrium as shown in Figure 7.5. Compare the thickness of the atrium wall with the ventricle wall. Using a ruler, measure the maximum thickness of the walls of the left atrium and ventricle and record them in the Results section.

6   Repeat the procedure for the right ventricle and atrium, again measuring the maximum thickness of the right atrium and ventricle, and record them in the Results section.

7   Now that the heart is fully opened, the bicuspid and tricuspid valves should be clear. The bicuspid and tricuspid valves are composed of thin tissue that are attached to the heart with tendons. Draw a sketch of one of the valves showing the tendons. The semilunar valves should also be visible inside the arteries – try to draw one of these, illustrating the pocket-like structure in the Results section.

TIP

When cutting with a scalpel, use repeated light sweeps rather than 'sawing' at the heart.

Results

Bicuspid or tricuspid valve	Semilunar valve

Maximum thickness of right atrium: ....

Maximum thickness of left atrium: ....

Maximum thickness of right ventricle: ....

Maximum thickness of left ventricle: ....

Analysis, conclusion and evaluation

a i   Explain the difference in thickness of the left and right ventricle walls.

....

....

....

ii   Is there a significant difference in the thickness of the left and right atrium walls? If not, why is there no difference?

....

....

....

iii   Suggest whether the volumes of the right and left ventricles are the same.

....

....

....

b i   Explain the general function of the heart valves.

....

....

....

ii   State the role of the tendons attached to the bicuspid and tricuspid valves.

....

....

....

iii   Suggest how the semilunar valves carry out their function.

....

....

....

Practical Investigation 7.3: Observing and drawing the different structures of arteries, veins and capillaries

Arteries, veins and capillaries have very different functions, and this is explained by the differences in their structures. Arteries need to carry blood under high pressure away from the heart, whilst veins return blood that is under much lower pressure back to the heart. Whilst it is essential that neither arteries nor veins have permeable walls, the function of capillaries is to carry out the exchange of substances between the blood and tissues – this requires capillaries to be thin and permeable.

YOU WILL NEED

Equipment:

- light microscope • prepared sections of TS arteries, veins and capillaries
- pencil, HB or 2H grade • eraser • pencil sharpener • ruler • eyepiece graticule • stage micrometer

Safety considerations

- Make sure you have read the Safety advice section at the beginning of this book and listen to any advice from your teacher before carrying out this investigation.

Method

1 Set up the light microscope as you did in Chapter 1.

2 Take the prepared slide (or slides) and using low power, bring the blood vessels into focus.

3 Identify the artery – this will have a more regular, circular structure with a thicker wall and smaller lumen.

4 Identify the vein – this will have a less regular structure and is often flattened, the wall will be thinner but the lumen may be wider.

5 Try to identify a capillary – this may not be easy as they are very small and will depend upon the quality of the section (Figure 7.6 shows an artery and a vein).

6 Change the objective lens to the higher power objective to look more closely at the three blood vessels.

7 Focus on the artery and draw a cross-section in the Results section, identifying the following tissues:

- inner layer (thin endothelium on the inside)
- middle layer (thick layer containing elastic fibres, collagen and smooth muscle)
- outer layer (thick layer containing some collagen fibres and elastic fibres)
- lumen (the space in the centre)

> **TIP**
>
> The fibrous nature of the external and middle layers should be clear, although it may be difficult to see exactly where the border between the two is.

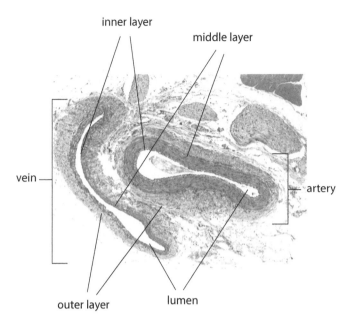

inner layer

middle layer

vein

artery

outer layer

lumen

Figure 7.6: Photomicrograph of transverse section of an artery and vein.

8 Use the eyepiece graticule and stage micrometer, as explained in Chapter 1, to measure the thickness of the artery wall and the diameter of the lumen. Record these in the Results section and include a scale bar on your diagram of the artery.

9 Focus on the vein and draw a cross-section in the Results section, identifying the following tissues:

- inner layer (thin endothelium on the inside)

- middle layer (thin layer containing elastic fibres and smooth muscle)

- outer layer (thin layer mostly containing some collagen fibres)

- lumen (the space in the centre)

10 Use the eyepiece graticule and stage micrometer to measure the thickness of the vein wall and the maximum diameter of the lumen. Record these in the Results section and include a scale bar on your diagram of the vein.

> **TIP**
>
> The wall of the vein will be much thinner than the artery and the shape should be less regular.

Results

TS artery	TS vein

Blood vessel	Thickness of wall / μm	Maximum thickness of lumen / μm
artery		
vein		
capillary*	(one cell thick endothelium, approx. 1 μm)	approx. 10

Table 7.3: Comparison of features.

*Capillaries have been included for comparison.

Analysis, conclusion and evaluation

a   Describe the differences in the structures of the artery, vein and capillary.

    ....

    ....

    ....

b   Arteries branch into smaller vessels called arterioles. Arterioles control the flow
    of blood to organs and tissues by dilating and constricting. Figure 7.7 shows the
    proportions of the tissues found in the walls of an artery and an arteriole.

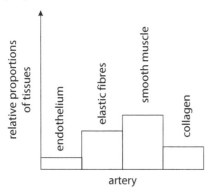

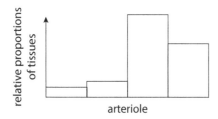

Figure 7.7: Proportion of different tissues in the walls of arteries and arterioles.

Describe how the structure of the wall of the arteriole differs from the artery and explain how this enables it to carry out its function.

....

....

....

....

c   Use your results and your own knowledge to explain how the artery, vein and capillary are adapted to their functions.

....

....

....

....

....

....

d   Figure 7.8 shows the velocity and pressure of blood in different blood vessels along with the total cross-sectional area of blood vessels.

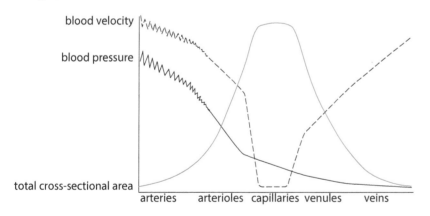

Figure 7.8: Velocity, pressure and total cross-sectional area of blood vessels.

i   Describe the changes in velocity, pressure and cross-sectional area as the blood moves from arteries to veins.

....

....

....

....

ii Explain the changes in cross-sectional area.

....

....

....

....

iii Explain why the blood pressure changes – the formula for pressure is:

    pressure = force (from heart contraction) ÷ area

....

....

....

....

iv Explain why the velocity of blood changes (you will also have to think about how blood is moved through veins).

....

....

....

....

Practical Investigation 7.4: Observing and drawing the structure of the respiratory system and its tissues

In this practical your teacher will show you the anatomy of the respiratory system of a sheep. You will observe and draw sections through the trachea, bronchi, bronchioles and alveoli. It should help you to develop a good understanding of the anatomy of these structures and how they are adapted for their functions.

YOU WILL NEED

Equipment:

- light microscope • prepared sections of TS trachea, bronchi, bronchiole, alveoli • pencil, HB or 2H grade • eraser • pencil sharpener • ruler
- eyepiece graticule • stage micrometer

Safety considerations

- Make sure you have read the Safety advice section at the beginning of this book and listen to any advice from your teacher before carrying out this investigation.

- For the observation of the sections, standard laboratory safety rules should be followed.

Method

Part 1: Observing the dissection of the respiratory system

Your teacher will show you the overall anatomy of the respiratory system. During the demonstration, you should make diagrams and take notes about certain features and adaptations that your teacher points out. These should be recorded in the following space. You should include aspects such as:

- overall appearance of lungs: colour, texture, elasticity, pleural membranes

- trachea: shape and function of the cartilage, diameter

- bronchi: shape and function of the cartilage, diameter

- terminal bronchioles: shape and function, absence of cartilage, diameter

Part 2: Observation and plan drawing of the structure of trachea, bronchi, bronchioles and alveoli

1   Set up the light microscope as you did in Chapter 1.

2   Take the prepared slide of TS trachea and using low power, bring it into focus.

3   Change the objective lens to high power and focus on one section of the wall. Use Figure 7.9 to help you identify tissues on your section. The photomicrograph shows a section of trachea wall. Ciliated epithelia with goblet cells within it are clearly visible. Underneath the ciliated epithelia are layers of smooth muscle and loose connective tissue. The thick block of cartilage is underneath the smooth muscle layer.

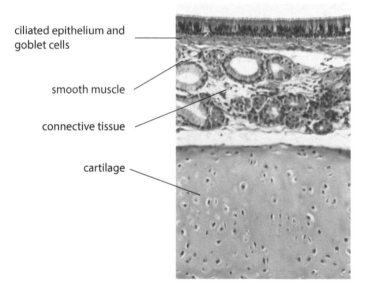

ciliated epithelium and goblet cells

smooth muscle

connective tissue

cartilage

Figure 7.9: Photomicrograph of transverse section of trachea.

You should be able to see:

- a layer of ciliated epithelia – the cilia may not be very clear

- goblet cells that are found between epithelium cells. These may be stained a different colour

- a layer of smooth muscle under the epithelium

- an area of loose tissue that has blood vessels and mucus glands present

- a thick section of cartilage tissue.

4   Draw a plan diagram of a section of the wall of the trachea in the following space, labelling all the structures listed. Remember not to try to draw individual cells. If you can see them, draw a small section of tissue next to your diagram to show a few individual ciliated epithelium and goblet cells.

5   Change the slide to one of TS bronchus and again view a section of the wall using the high-power objective lens. Figure 7.10 shows a photomicrograph of a section of bronchus wall. The upper surface is ciliated epithelia with a few goblet cells present. Underneath this is a layer of connective tissue and smooth muscle, and underneath this is a layer of cartilage.

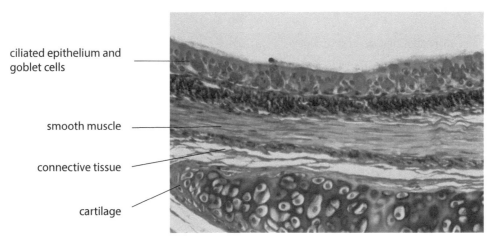

ciliated epithelium and goblet cells

smooth muscle

connective tissue

cartilage

Figure 7.10: Photomicrograph of section of bronchus wall.

6 Draw a plan diagram of a section of bronchus wall (using Figure 7.10 to help you) labelling:

- ciliated epithelium – this may be thinner than in the trachea

- goblet cells – there may be fewer than in the trachea

- a layer of smooth muscle under the epithelium

- a thinner area of loose tissue with fewer blood vessels and mucus glands than the trachea

- a section of cartilage tissue – this will be as a block rather than a ring.

> TIP
>
> Remember to draw what you can see and not what you want to see!

7   Once you have finished this diagram, change the slide to one of TS bronchiole and again view a section of the wall using the high-power objective lens.

8   The bronchiole will be much thinner than the bronchus, there will be no cartilage and it will have a slightly different structure. The epithelium may be folded. Figure 7.11 shows a photomicrograph of a transverse section of lung tissue. The folded layer of ciliated epithelia is clear, surrounding it is a circular layer of smooth muscle. The bronchiole is surrounded by alveoli.

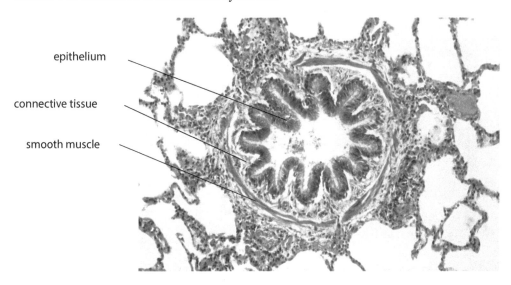

epithelium

connective tissue

smooth muscle

Figure 7.11: Photomicrograph of transverse section of lung tissue.

9   Draw a plan diagram of a section of lung tissue (using Figure 7.11 to help you), labelling:

*   epithelium – this may be some ciliated cells but no goblet cells

*   a thin layer of connective tissue surrounding the epithelium

*   a layer of smooth muscle surrounding the connective tissue.

10 Change the slide to one of TS alveolus and view a section of the wall using the high-power objective lens.

11 The alveoli will be visible as large spaces separated by thin layers of squamous epithelium. Blood vessels and bronchioles may also be present. Figure 7.12 shows a photomicrograph of a section of lung tissue. The squamous epithelium layers of several alveoli are clear.

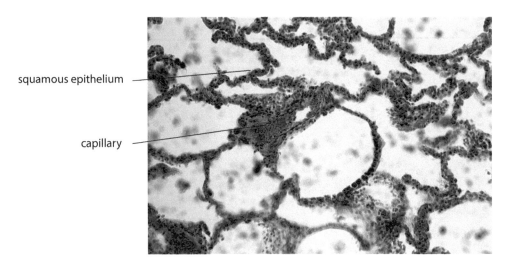

Figure 7.12: Photomicrograph of transverse section of alveolus.

12 Draw a plan diagram of a section showing several alveoli (using Figure 7.12 to help you), labelling:

- alveoli

- squamous epithelium

- capillaries (and other blood vessels).

Analysis, conclusion and evaluation

a   Complete Table 7.4 by adding 'yes' or 'no' to describe the presence or absence of different cell and tissue types.

Airway	Cartilage	Ciliated epithelium	Goblet cells	Smooth muscle
trachea				
bronchus				
bronchiole				
alveolus				

Table 7.4: Comparison of features.

b   Figure 7.13 **a** shows some normal human alveoli and **b** shows some alveoli from the lung of a smoker. Both images have the same magnification (×75).

a   b

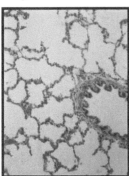 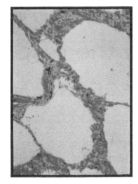

Figure 7.13: Photomicrograph of a) normal alveoli b) alveoli from the lung of a smoker.

i   Describe the differences in the structures shown in Figure 7.13a and 7.13b.

   ....

   ....

ii   State the name of the disease that is illustrated by Figure 7.13b and explain the effects on the patient.

   ....

   ....

> Chapter 8
Energy and respiration

CHAPTER OUTLINE

This chapter relates to Chapter 12: Energy and respiration, in the Coursebook.
In this chapter, you will complete practical investigations on:

- 8.1 Using a simple respirometer to calculate the respiratory quotient of germinating seeds
- 8.2 The effect of temperature on the rate of respiration of an invertebrate
- 8.3 The effect of glucose concentration on the respiration rate of yeast using a redox indicator
- 8.4 The ability of yeast to use different sugars during fermentation

Practical Investigation 8.1: Using a simple respirometer to calculate the respiratory quotient of germinating seeds

Respiratory quotients (RQ)

The respiratory quotient (RQ) is a measure used to compare the rate of oxygen uptake and rate of carbon dioxide production. It is defined as the ratio of carbon dioxide evolved to oxygen consumed and is calculated using the equation:

RQ = volume of carbon dioxide evolved ÷ volume of oxygen consumed

The RQ of an organism can give a hint of the substrate used for respiration and whether respiration is totally aerobic or some anaerobic respiration is occurring. For example, during the aerobic respiration of glucose, the number of molecules of carbon dioxide produced is the same as the number of molecules of oxygen used:

$$C_6H_{12}O_6 + 6O_2 \rightarrow 6CO_2 + 6H_2O$$
$$\text{The RQ} = 6 \div 6$$
$$= 1.0$$

In reality, some of the respiration will be aerobic and some anaerobic and so the RQ will be higher than 1.0.

If the fatty acid, oleic acid, is the substrate, the equation is:

$$C_{18}H_{34}O_2 + 25.5\,O_2 \rightarrow 18\,CO_2 + 17\,H_2O$$
$$\text{The RQ} = 18 \div 25.5$$
$$= 0.7$$

If glucose undergoes alcoholic fermentation in the absence of oxygen, the equation is:

$$C_6H_{12}O_6 \rightarrow 2C_2H_5OH + 2CO_2$$

$$RQ = 2 \div 0$$

$$= \infty$$

Respirometers

A respirometer is a piece of equipment that is used to measure the respiration rate of a living organism by determining the rate of oxygen consumption. It can also be used to measure the rate of carbon dioxide evolution. There is a range of designs of respirometer available, some are very simple, some are more complicated; a typical one is shown in Figure 8.1. Key features include:

- a U-tube manometer with scale filled with dyed fluid. This is to measure the volume of oxygen used.

- a three-way tap and clamps to seal off the external air or reset the level of fluid using the syringe. If the equipment has a leak, the fluid will not move.

- a gauze platform or cradle to place the organism.

- soda lime (or KOH or NaOH) in the base of the boiling tubes. This will absorb carbon dioxide gas. As the organism uses up a volume of oxygen, this will be replaced by a volume of carbon dioxide which is then absorbed by the soda lime. This results in a net change in volume (usually a reduction) and so the pressure in the boiling tube reduces, drawing the fluid towards the boiling tube containing the living organism.

- a control tube with a mass of glass beads that is equal to the mass of living organism. This takes account of any volume changes of gas due to temperature changes.

- Different styles of respirometer may be used, your teacher will explain which one you will be using. Figure 8.1 shows two different styles: **a** has a control tube containing glass beads and uses a manometer; and **b** has no control and is a simpler form of respirometer.

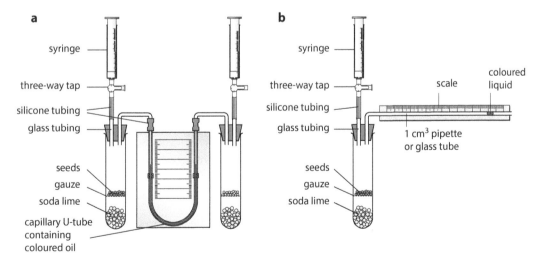

Figure 8.1: Two types of respirometer.

> ## YOU WILL NEED
>
> **Equipment:**
> • four boiling tubes • two U-tube respirometers filled with fluid • four bungs containing connecting tubes • glass beads, 20 g • soda lime granules, 20 g • two three-way taps • two screw clips • germinating seeds (mung beans or similar), 20 g • four wire gauzes or cradles • two sets of clamps, bosses and stands • boiling tube racks • eye protection • glass marker pen • 30 mm ruler or scale • two syringes, 1 cm³
>
> **Access to:**
> • balance

Safety considerations

- Make sure you have read the Safety advice section at the beginning of this book and listen to any advice from your teacher before carrying out this investigation.

- The glass capillary and delivery tubes break easily. Bungs and tubes should not be 'forced' and care should be taken when putting silicon tubing onto the ends of the glass delivery tubing.

- Soda lime is caustic and can cause severe burns. It is particularly dangerous to the eyes. Weigh it out carefully and if you spill any, clear it up. Eye protection must be worn and if you splash on skin, wash with water. If it is splashed in eyes, wash the eyes with gently running tap water for 20 min and seek medical attention.

- Seeds that are non-toxic and non-allergenic should be used.

Method

This method is for a U-tube manometer style of respirometer and your teacher will adapt it if you are using a different style of respirometer.

1 Place 5 g of soda lime into two boiling tubes.

2 Place a cradle or gauze into both boiling tubes above the soda lime.

3 Weigh out approximately 5 g of germinating seeds and place them into one of the boiling tubes. Record the exact mass.

4 Weigh out an equal mass of glass beads and place them into the other boiling tube (this is the control tube).

5 Place the bungs with the connecting tubes into the boiling tubes securely so that there are no leaks. Do not attach the three-way taps yet.

6 Clamp the U-tube manometer securely and then attach the connecting tubes from the boiling tubes, as shown in Figure 8.1.

7 Insert the 1 cm³ syringes into the three-way taps and check that the tap has the syringe 'closed'.

8 Attach the three-way tap and syringes as shown in Figure 8.1 and turn the taps to seal the apparatus (close off the external air). Use the syringes to make the fluid in the manometer level. Record the position of the fluid on the scale of the U-tube manometer using a pencil or pen.

9   Set up a second experiment exactly the same but with no soda lime in the boiling tubes.

10 Record the distance that the manometer fluid has travelled after 24 and 48 h (or approximately if these exact times are not possible) in Table 8.1. Use the syringe to reset the level of the fluid each time it is measured.

11 Record the internal diameter of the U-tube manometer.

Results

Time period / h	Distance moved by fluid during 24 h period / mm		
	with soda lime	without soda lime	with soda lime – without soda lime
24			
48			

Table 8.1: Results table.

Internal diameter of U-tube manometer: ....

Exact mass of seeds used: ....

Analysis, conclusion and evaluation

Calculating the rate of oxygen consumption

To calculate the rate of oxygen consumption in $mm^3\,hr^{-1}$ per g seed mass, you will need to perform the following calculations:

a   The volume of oxygen used approximates to the volume of a cylinder of the U-tube manometer:

$$V = \pi r^2 d$$

where d = the distance moved by the fluid

r = internal radius of the U-tube manometer

Now, calculate the volumes of oxygen used by the seeds with soda lime during each of the 24 h periods, and record the values in Table 8.2.

b   To calculate the rate of oxygen consumption in $mm^3\,h^{-1}$ divide the volumes of oxygen you have calculated by the time period of 24 h.

rate of oxygen consumption = volume of oxygen ÷ time taken

Record the values in Table 8.2.

c   To calculate the rate of oxygen production per gram of seeds, divide the rate of oxygen consumption you have calculated by the mass of seeds.

rate of oxygen consumption per gram of seed = rate of oxygen consumption ÷ mass of seed

Record the values in Table 8.2.

Calculating the rate of carbon dioxide evolution

To calculate the rate of carbon dioxide evolution, we need to compare the movement of the fluid in the experiments with soda lime against the experiments without soda lime. If there is no soda lime present, the carbon dioxide produced will force the fluid back out again. If aerobic respiration of glucose occurs, six moles of oxygen will be replaced by six moles of carbon dioxide and the fluid will not move.

d   Calculate the difference in distances moved by the fluid with and without soda lime and record them in Table 8.1.

e   Now use your values to calculate the volumes of carbon dioxide evolved, the rates of carbon dioxide production and the rates of carbon dioxide production per gram of seed for each time period. Record your results in Table 8.2.

Time period / h	Oxygen			Carbon dioxide		
	Volume consumed / mm^3	Rate of consumption / $mm^3\,h^{-1}$	Rate of consumption per mass of seed / $mm^3\,h^{-1}$ per gram	Volume evolved / mm^3	Rate of evolution / $mm^3\,h^{-1}$	Rate of evolution per mass of seed / $mm^3\,h^{-1}$ per gram
0–24						
24–48						

Table 8.2: Results table.

Calculating the respiratory quotients

f   You can now calculate the respiratory quotient (RQ) for each time period using the formula:

RQ = rate of evolution of carbon dioxide per gram ÷ rate of consumption of oxygen

RQ between 0 and 24 h: ....

RQ between 24 and 48 h: ....

Table 8.3 shows the respiratory quotients for the aerobic respiration of different substrates.

Respiratory substrate	Respiratory quotient (RQ)
carbohydrate	1.0
lipid	0.7
protein	0.9

Table 8.3: Respiratory quotients for different substrates.

TIP

difference in fluid distance = distance moved by fluid with soda lime – distance moved without soda lime

---

g Use the information in Table 8.3 to explain your calculated RQ values for both time periods. You should consider if the substrate changes during germination.

....

....

....

h Explain how your results and conclusions would be affected if the concentration of oxygen in the boiling tube had become very low.

....

....

....

i Explain why it is important to calculate the rates of oxygen consumption and carbon dioxide evolution per gram of seeds.

....

....

....

j Temperature was not standardised in the experiment. Would this influence the calculated value of RQ?

....

....

....

k No leaves would be present after 48 h. If the experiment were to be conducted for a longer period of time, the tubes would be wrapped in foil. Explain why this is necessary to provide valid results.

....

....

....

Practical Investigation 8.2: The effect of temperature on the rate of respiration of an invertebrate

This investigation is in two parts. In the first part, you will plan an investigation into the effect of temperature on the rate of respiration using respirometers, whilst in the second part, you will carry out the practical work and statistical analysis.

Respiration, like most of the chemical reactions in living things, is controlled by enzymes and so is affected by temperature. Invertebrates, such as blowfly larvae and woodlice, have a body temperature that is determined by the environmental temperature. If the environmental temperature changes, it will affect the rate of respiration in the cells of invertebrates.

Planning

The first thing that you will need to do is formulate a **hypothesis** about the effect of temperature on the rate of respiration.

In science, a hypothesis is an idea or explanation that you test through study and experimentation. When you formulate it, you should make a statement in terms of what you expect the effect of changing the independent variable will be on the dependent variable. You should also give a reason as to why you think the hypothesis is correct.

Formulate a hypothesis for the effect of temperature on the respiration rate of invertebrates and justify your hypothesis using your knowledge of enzymes and biochemical reactions.

hypothesis:

....

....

....

reason:

....

....

....

....

KEY WORD
hypothesis: a hypothesis assumes there is no relationship between two variables, or that there is no significant difference between two samples

Now that you have formulated a hypothesis, you need to plan a method that will test it. Follow the steps below to help you plan your method.

Variables

In this experiment, the independent variable is the temperature and the dependent variable is the rate of oxygen consumption.

Independent variable

- Decide on the range of temperatures that you will use and the increments. You should select five appropriate temperatures that are evenly spread.

- State how many replicates you will carry out to generate reliable results.

- Explain what equipment you will use and how you will change the independent variable.

Temperatures: ....

Number of repeats for each temperature: ....

Method for changing and maintaining temperature: ....

....

....

....

Dependent variable

- Explain how you will accurately and reliably measure the dependent variable (the volume of oxygen consumption). As you are determining a rate, you will need to consider what you will measure and a reference to a timeframe.

- To compare the rates, you should calculate the oxygen consumption per gram of invertebrate.

- Method for determining rate of oxygen consumption in $mm^3 \, min^{-1}$ per gram of invertebrate:

....

....

Standardised variables

List variables that will affect the rate of oxygen consumption and suggest practical methods for keeping them constant. It is not always possible to keep some variables constant but some form of monitoring should be carried out to see if there were fluctuations during the investigation.

> **TIP**
>
> As you are using living animals, you will need to consider ethics and ensure that:
>
> - a temperature range is used that will not stress or harm the animals
>
> - other strategies are used to ensure that the animals do not experience unnecessary stress (rest period, ensuring that air is refreshed so that they do not suffocate).

Standardised variables and methods for keeping them constant / monitoring them:

....

....

....

....

....

....

YOU WILL NEED

List the equipment you will need:

- • ....
- • ....
- • ....
- • ....
- • ....
- • ....

- • ....
- • ....
- • ....
- • ....
- • ....
- • ....

Safety considerations

List any safety considerations that you need to consider:

....

....

....

....

....

Risk assessment

It is critical to assess risks and give suggestions for how to reduce these risks. You should consider:

- chemicals that you are using

- techniques that you are using that may carry a risk (such as using scalpels, Bunsen burners or hot water)

- living organisms that may carry disease or a risk of allergy.

You will sometimes need to do a bit of research when using chemicals or living organisms. Complete Table 8.4.

Risk	Methods to minimise risk

Table 8.4: Results table.

TIP

Safety considerations can include things like ensuring that the three-way tap is set to the correct position.

Method

Now, use the summaries that you have made above to write a full written step-by-step plan as to what you intend to do explaining exactly how you will carry out the investigation. It can be written in bullet points and should be detailed enough for another researcher to use it without any other help.

....

....

....

....

....

....

....

....

....

....

....

....

....

....

....

....

....

....

Results

Record your results in Table 8.5.

Temperature / °C	Distance moved by fluid in manometer / mm			
	0–5 min	5–10 min	10–15 min	mean
10				
15				
20				
25				
30				
35				

Table 8.5: Results table.

Mass of invertebrates: .... g

Internal diameter of U-tube manometer: .... mm

Analysis, conclusion and evaluation

Calculating the rate of oxygen consumption per minute per gram of invertebrate

a   Calculate the mean distance moved by fluid in the manometer tube for each temperature and record your answers in Table 8.5. If any of the repeat values appear to be anomalous, they should be left out when calculating the mean.

b   We can assume that the volume of oxygen consumed by the invertebrates approximates to the volume of a cylinder within the manometer. Using the formula for the volume of a cylinder, calculate the volumes of mean oxygen consumed in cubic millimetres and record them in Table 8.6.

$$V = \pi r^2 d$$

where:

r = internal radius of the manometer

d = the mean distance moved by the fluid

Temperature / °C	Mean volume of oxygen consumed in 5 min / mm³	Mean rate of oxygen consumption / mm³ min⁻¹	Mean rate of oxygen consumption per gram of invertebrate / mm³ min⁻¹ per gram of invertebrate
10			
15			
20			
25			
30			
35			

Table 8.6: Calculated results table.

c   Calculate the rates of oxygen consumption per minute by dividing the mean volume of oxygen consumed in 5 min by five. Record your answers in Table 8.6.

d   Calculate the rates of oxygen consumption per minute per gram of invertebrate by dividing the mean rate of oxygen consumption per minute by the mass of invertebrates. Record your answers in Table 8.6.

Displaying the results as a graph

e   Both the independent and dependent variables are **continuous variables**. It is likely that the oxygen consumption rates at untested temperatures would follow the trend of the known temperatures. The correct graph to plot will have temperature on the x-axis, mean rate of oxygen consumption per gram of invertebrate on the y-axis and a best-fit line (or curve) should be drawn if appropriate.

TIP

You do not need to start the axes at zero. Choose a scale that allows the plots to cover over half of the graph paper and choose sensible increments so that it is easy to plot and read points that are not on major gridlines.

KEY WORD

continuous variables: variables that are quantitative and can have any value within an interval; for example, length or mass are continuous variables

Carrying out a statistical test

In this investigation, we are looking to see if there is a **correlation** between temperature and mean rate of oxygen consumption. There are two statistical tests that can be used to test for a significant correlation:

Pearson's linear correlation – to establish if there is a linear relationship between two variables

Spearman's rank correlation – to establish if there is a correlation (not necessarily linear) between two paired sets of data.

f   Because the relationship may not necessarily be linear, you will carry out a Spearman's rank correlation test using the following steps:

  i   Enter your pairs of data for each temperature and the corresponding mean rate of oxygen consumption in Table 8.7.

  ii   Rank the temperatures in order from highest (rank 1) to lowest (rank 6) and record the ranks (R_t) in Table 8.7.

  iii   Rank the mean rate of oxygen consumption from highest (rank 1) to lowest (rank 6) and record the ranks (R_o) in Table 8.7.

  iv   Calculate the difference in rank ($Rt - Ro$), D, for each pair and record these in Table 8.7.

  v   Calculate the square of the difference of each rank (D^2), and record these in Table 8.7.

  vi   Add together all the values for D^2 to find ΣD^2 and record this in Table 8.7.

  vii   The formula for calculating Spearman's rank correlation coefficient is:

$$r_s = 1 - \left(\frac{6\Sigma d^2}{n^3 - n} \right)$$

where:

rS is Spearman's rank coefficient

ΣD^2 is the sum of the differences between the ranks of the two data sets

n is the number of data sets

Use your values of ΣD^2 and n to calculate r_s.

<table>
<tr><td>Temperature / °C</td><td>Rank for temperature, R_t</td><td>Rate of oxygen consumption / mm³ min⁻¹ per gram</td><td>Rank for oxygen consumption, R_o</td><td>Difference in ranks, D ($R_t - R_o$)</td><td>D^2</td></tr>
<tr><td></td><td></td><td></td><td></td><td></td><td></td></tr>
<tr><td></td><td></td><td></td><td></td><td></td><td></td></tr>
<tr><td></td><td></td><td></td><td></td><td></td><td></td></tr>
<tr><td></td><td></td><td></td><td></td><td></td><td></td></tr>
<tr><td></td><td></td><td></td><td></td><td></td><td></td></tr>
<tr><td></td><td></td><td></td><td></td><td></td><td></td></tr>
<tr><td></td><td></td><td></td><td></td><td>$\Sigma D^2 =$ ....</td><td></td></tr>
</table>

Table 8.7: Calculated results table.

KEY WORDS

correlation: a relationship, or connection, between two variables. Correlations may be positive (if one variable increases so does the other) or negative (if one variable increases, the other decreases.)

Pearson's linear correlation: a statistical test used to determine whether two variables show a linear correlation

Spearman's rank correlation: a statistical test to determine whether two variables are correlated

$r_s = $ ....

If the calculated value of r_s is positive, it indicates a positive correlation; if it is negative, it indicates a negative correlation.

viii The calculated value of r_s is the correlation coefficient. The closer the value is to 1, the more likely that there is a genuine correlation between the two sets of data. To establish whether a correlation is significant, you now need to compare the value of r_s with a critical value from Table 8.8.

n	5	6	7	8	9	10	11	12
Critical value of r_s at the 0.05 probability level	1.00	0.89	0.79	0.76	0.68	0.65	0.60	0.54

Table 8.8: Critical values of r_s.

As in most statistical tests used in biology, the probability of 0.05 is the baseline. If your calculated value is greater than the critical value, there is a probability of 0.05 or less that the correlation is due to chance. This means that there is a significant correlation, so we reject the null hypothesis. If the calculated value is less than the critical value, there is not a significant correlation.

Delete the appropriate words in *italic* type:

The calculated value of r_s is (*greater than* / *less than*) the critical value.

This means that there is (*a significant correlation* / *no significant correlation*) between temperature and mean rate of oxygen consumption.

g Write a conclusion for your results. You should include the following:

- a description of the patterns and how strong any correlation is

- an explanation of what the results show. If there is an increase in rate of oxygen concentration with increasing temperature, explain why this has occurred.

....

....

....

....

....

....

....

h   Look at your raw data and identify any results that are possibly anomalous (in other words, do not fit the trend). Suggest possible reasons for the anomalies.

....

....

....

....

....

i   Comment on the strength and validity of your conclusion. You should comment on how close the points fit your best-fit line or curve and what the statistics show. To be valid, there should have been sufficient replicates that show a similar pattern and all other variables should have been standardised.

....

....

....

....

....

....

....

....

j   Compare your results with other groups. Comment on whether they show similar patterns.

....

....

....

....

....

k List any possible systematic and random errors that may have occurred.

systematic errors:

....

....

random errors:

....

....

Practical Investigation 8.3: The effect of glucose concentration on the respiration rate of yeast using a redox indicator

Redox indicators such as 2,6-dichlorophenolindophenol (DCPIP) and methylene blue are often used to detect oxidation and reduction reactions. When both these substances accept electrons (or hydrogen), that is, are reduced, they change colour from blue to colourless (see Figure 8.2). Both are blue in their oxidised state. As they do not damage cells, they can be used to determine respiration rates of yeast by recording the time taken to change from blue to colourless.

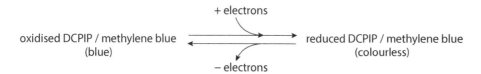

Figure 8.2: Colour change associated with oxidation / reduction of DCPIP.

In this practical, you will investigate the effect of changing the concentration of glucose on the rate of respiration of yeast using methylene blue as an indicator.

> **YOU WILL NEED**
>
> **Equipment:**
> • 12 test tubes • two large beakers, 500 cm³ • Bunsen burner, tripod and gauze or source of hot and cold water (thermostatically controlled water baths may be used) • pipettes or syringes, 1 cm³, 5 cm³, 10 cm³ • thermometer • 0.005% methylene blue solution, 20 cm³ • 10% glucose solution, 25 cm³ • distilled water, 100 cm³ • yeast suspension, 100 cm³ • boiled yeast suspension, 10 cm³ • timer • bungs for test tubes • glass marker pen

Safety considerations

• Make sure you have read the Safety advice section at the beginning of this book and listen to any advice from your teacher before carrying out this investigation.

• Take care when using Bunsen burners.

• Methylene blue is classed as harmful and may be an irritant. If you splash any on skin, wash it off. Eye protection should be worn. If you splash any in your eye, wash your eye with water.

• Glucose carries a low risk.

• Yeast is a living microbe so wear laboratory coats and wash hands after the experiment.

Method

1 Set up water baths at a temperature of between 35 and 40°C using the large beakers, Bunsen burner, tripod and gauze. Use the thermometer to check and maintain the temperatures.

2 Label six test tubes 1–6.

3 Use a pipette to place 2 cm³ yeast suspension into test tubes 1–5. Make sure that you shake the suspension as the yeast will settle down to the bottom. Place the tubes into the water bath.

4 Place 2 cm³ boiled yeast suspension into test tube 6. Place the tube into the water bath.

5 Label six more test tubes 1–6. Using a pipette, add 2 cm³ methylene blue solution to each test tube. Add 10% glucose and distilled water to each tube in the proportions shown in Table 8.9. Place the test tubes into a water bath.

Test-tube number	Glucose concentration / %	Volume of 10% glucose / cm³	Volume of distilled water / cm³
1	0.0	0.0	0.0
2	2.5	0.5	1.5
3	5.0	1.0	1.0
4	7.5	1.5	0.5
5	10.0	2.0	0.0
6	10.0	2.0	0.0

Table 8.9: Method for preparation of glucose solutions.

6 Leave the test tubes in the water baths for 10 min.

7 After 10 min, pour the methylene blue / glucose mixtures into the corresponding test tubes containing the yeast suspensions. The contents of the test tube labelled '1' with the methylene blue needs to be poured into the test tube labelled '1' that contains the yeast suspension.

8 Mix the contents thoroughly for about 20 s and return the test tubes to a water bath. Do not mix or shake the tubes again. Record the time taken for the blue colour to disappear in each tube in Table 8.10.

9 The experiment should be repeated two more times. This can be done by shaking the tubes until the blue colour returns.

Results

Test-tube number	Glucose concentration / %	Time taken for blue colour to disappear / s			
		1	2	3	mean
1	0.0				
2	2.5				
3	5.0				
4	7.5				
5	10.0				
6	10.0*				

Table 8.10: Results table.

*Test tube 6 contained boiled yeast.

Analysis, conclusion and evaluation

a Calculate the mean times taken for the blue colour to disappear and record these in Table 8.10.

b Plot an appropriate graph to show the effect of glucose concentration on time taken for the methylene blue to change colour. (Ignore test tube 6 with boiled yeast.)

c Describe the pattern shown by your graph.

....

....

....

d **i** Use your knowledge of respiration to explain why the methylene blue changed colour.

....

....

....

    ii Explain the effects of increasing the concentration of glucose on the time taken for the blue colour to disappear.

....

....

....

e Explain the purpose of test tube 6 in the experiment.

....

....

....

f Suggest why the blue colour disappeared in the methylene blue in the test tube with no added glucose.

....

....

....

g **i** Explain why shaking the tubes returned the colour of the methylene blue to blue.

....

....

....

ii Explain why you were told to not mix or shake the mixtures during the experiment.

....

....

....

h Evaluate the reliability of this practical.

....

....

....

....

....

....

Practical Investigation 8.4: The ability of yeast to use different sugars during fermentation

Yeast (*Saccharomyces cerevisiae*) is able to use different carbohydrate sugars as a substrate during fermentation. Carbon dioxide gas is released during fermentation and so the rate of carbon dioxide production can be used as a measure of the rate of fermentation. In this practical, you will measure the rate of carbon dioxide production by yeast when using different sugars for fermentation.

YOU WILL NEED

Equipment:
- five test tubes • five fermentation tubes • Bunsen burner, tripod and gauze or source of hot and cold water (thermostatically controlled water baths may be used) • large beaker, 250 cm^3 • 0.25 mol dm^{-3} glucose solution, 10 cm^3
- 0.25 mol dm^{-3} fructose solution, 10 cm^3 • 0.25 mol dm^{-3} sucrose solution, 10 cm^3 • 0.25 mol dm^{-3} maltose solution, 10 cm^3 • distilled water, 10 cm^3
- pipettes or syringes, 1, 5, 10 cm^3 • thermometer • yeast suspension, 25 cm^3
- timer

Safety considerations

- Make sure you have read the Safety advice section at the beginning of this book and listen to any advice from your teacher before carrying out this investigation.

- Take care when using Bunsen burners.

- Always wear eye protection.

- Glucose, fructose, sucrose and maltose carry a low risk.

- Yeast is a living microbe so wear laboratory coats and wash hands after the experiment.

Method

1   Label five test tubes 1–5.

2   Use the Bunsen burner, tripod and gauze to set up a water bath at between 35 and 40 °C.

3   Use a pipette to place 2 cm³ of yeast suspension into each test tube. Make sure that you shake the yeast suspension as the yeast will settle down to the bottom.

4   Use a pipette to place 2 cm³ 0.25 mol dm⁻³ glucose solution into test tube 1.

5   Use a pipette to place 2 cm³ 0.25 mol dm⁻³ fructose solution into test tube 2.

6   Use a pipette to place 2 cm³ 0.25 mol dm⁻³ sucrose solution into test tube 3.

7   Use a pipette to place 2 cm³ 0.25 mol dm⁻³ lactose solution into test tube 4.

8   Use a pipette to place 2 cm³ 0.25 mol dm⁻³ distilled water into test tube 5.

9   Place all the test tubes into the water bath for 5 min to reach the correct temperature.

10   Using a dropping pipette, remove some of the mixture from test tube 1 and use it to fill up a fermentation tube to the brim as shown in Figure 8.3. Part **a** shows the method for filling up the fermentation tube to the top; part **b** shows the inverted fermentation at start of experiment; and part **c** shows the fermentation tube during the experiment showing carbon dioxide gas trapped in the tube.

11   Hold the test tube at an angle, turn the fermentation tube upside-down and quickly slide it down into the test tube. If a bubble forms in the tube on the way down, remove it and refill it. Replace the test tube and fermentation tube into the water bath. Repeat for all the test tubes.

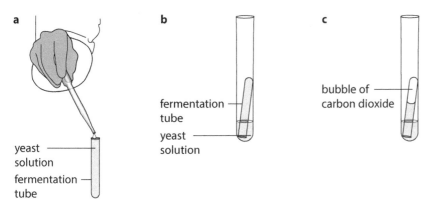

Figure 8.3: Method for investigation 8.4.

12 Bubbles should form at the top of the fermentation tubes. Record the length of the carbon dioxide bubble at intervals of 10 min in Table 8.11 for 60 min (the table should be extended if time allows).

Results

Test-tube number	Name of sugar	Length of bubble at time intervals / mm							
		10 min	20 min	30 min	40 min	50 min	60 min	70 min	80 min
1	glucose								
2	fructose								
3	sucrose								
4	maltose								
5	none								

Table 8.11: Results table.

Analysis, conclusion and evaluation

a   Draw a line graph to show the increasing length of bubble over time.

- You will need to place time on the *x*-axis and the length of the carbon dioxide bubble on the *y*-axis.

- Draw a separate line for each sugar (join points with straight lines) and include a key.

b Describe the patterns shown by your results in detail. You should compare each sugar (and water).

....

....

....

....

....

c Explain in as much detail as you can why the different sugars give different results.

....

....

....

....

....

d Explain why the solutions were incubated in the water bath for 5 min before placing a sample in the fermentation tubes.

....

....

....

e Explain how your graphs could be used to determine the maximum rates of carbon dioxide production.

....

....

....

> ⟩ Chapter 9

Photosynthesis

CHAPTER OUTLINE

This chapter relates to Chapter 13: Photosynthesis, in the Coursebook.

In this chapter, you will complete practical investigations on:

- 9.1 Identification and separation of photosynthetic pigments using paper chromatography

- 9.2 Effect of light intensity on the rate of photosynthesis

- 9.3 Gas exchange in a water plant

- 9.4 The effect of light wavelength on the light-dependent reaction (Hill reaction)

- 9.5 The effect of carbon dioxide concentration on rate of photosynthesis

---

Practical Investigation 9.1: Identification and separation of photosynthetic pigments using paper chromatography

Plants contain different primary and accessory pigments that all play a role in the absorption of light energy in photosynthesis. Most of the photosynthetic pigments (chlorophyll a, chlorophyll b, carotene, pheophytin and xanthophyll) are not very soluble in water and so need to be extracted using organic solvents. Paper **chromatography** is used to separate mixtures of solutes according to their solubility. More soluble compounds move further along the chromatogram than less soluble ones.

KEY WORD

chromatography: a method for the separation of a mixture of substances according to the speed with which they move through a medium, such as chromatography paper

---

YOU WILL NEED

Equipment:

- pestle and mortar • a small quantity of washed and dried sand • muslin cloth • test tube • glass capillary tube • chromatography paper, 80 mm long × 20 mm wide • boiling tube with cork bung • pin • hairdryer or fan • filter funnel • scissors • propanone, 50 cm³ • plant material • pipette, 5 cm³ or teat pipette • HB or 2H pencil • solvent (one part propanone : nine parts petroleum ether (boiling point 80–100 °C), 20 cm³ • pipette, 10 cm³, and pipette filler

Access to:

- centrifuge and two centrifuge tubes • powerful light source such as an overhead projector (OHP)

Safety considerations

- Make sure you have read the Safety advice section at the beginning of this book and listen to any advice from your teacher before carrying out this investigation.

- Propanone and petroleum ether are highly flammable and should not be used near any naked flame.

- Propanone and petroleum ether are classed as harmful. They should not be breathed in and eye protection should be worn at all times. If you spill anything, wash with water.

- Glass capillary tubes are easily broken. They should be handled carefully.

- Used solvents should not be poured down the sink but placed in a separate disposal bottle.

- Care should be taken when grinding the leaves.

Method

Part 1: Pigment extraction

1 Use the scissors to cut up approximately 10 g of fresh, green leaves and place the pieces into the mortar. Only use the leaves of the plant.

2 Add a very small amount of sand to the mortar and approximately 10 cm³ propanone.

3 Use the pestle to grind the leaves until a dark green, highly concentrated extract is produced. It may be necessary to add more propanone – this should be done carefully as it will dilute the extract and make it too weak to use.

4 Place the muslin cloth into the funnel and place the end of the funnel into the test tube, as shown in Figure 9.1. Pour the extract through the muslin cloth and collect the liquid in the test tube. Use the pestle to squeeze as much extract from the leaves as possible.

> **TIP**
>
> Do not add too much propanone otherwise your extract will be too dilute. Add it gradually!

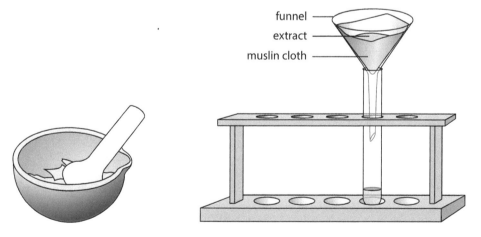

Figure 9.1: Apparatus for part 1 of investigation 9.1.

5 If a centrifuge is available, the extract should be centrifuged for approximately 2 min to remove all non-liquid material. If no centrifuge is available, the extract should be left for 5 min for the non-liquid material to drop.

6 Hold the extract in the test tube in a powerful beam of light, such as an OHP, and observe the appearance of the extract at 90°. Record the colour that the extract appears in the Results section.

Part 2: Chromatography

7 Cut a strip of chromatography paper so that it will almost (but not quite) reach the bottom of the boiling tube when the top is pinned into the cork bung (as shown in Figure 9.3).

8 Using a pencil, draw a straight line 20 mm from the bottom end of the paper.

9 Place the glass capillary tube in some of the pigment extract – some of the extract will be drawn up the tube. Then carefully place one spot on the centre of the pencil line of the chromatography paper as shown in Figure 9.2. The aim is to have a small spot of concentrated pigment extract – if the liquid spreads out through the filter paper, the concentration of pigment will be too low.

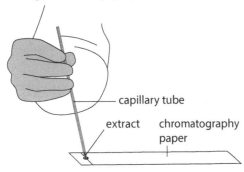

Figure 9.2: Method of applying sample to paper strip for part 2 of investigation 9.1.

10 Dry the spot on the filter paper. This may be done by using a hairdryer, a fan or by simply waving the paper in the air. When the spot is dry, add another amount of extract to exactly the same place. This should be repeated several times (drying it each time) until a dark green spot is present.

11 Use the pin to attach the chromatography paper to the bung, as shown in Figure 9.3. The paper should not touch the sides or bottom of the boiling tube it will be placed in.

12 Place approximately 5 cm³ of solvent into the boiling tube.

13 Carefully place the chromatography paper (attached to the bung) into the tube. Make sure that the pencil line does not go underneath the solvent and that you do not splash solvent up the boiling tube.

14 Place the boiling tube into a rack and leave it in a place where it will not be bumped. It may take 1–2 h to achieve a good separation of pigments – you will need to keep checking.

15 When the solvent has reached approximately 1 cm from the top, remove the chromatography paper and quickly mark the position the solvent has reached (the *solvent front*) with a pencil. Measure the distance the solvent has moved from the bottom pencil line and record it in the Results section.

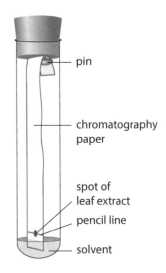

Figure 9.3: Apparatus for paper chromatography in part 2 of investigation 9.1.

16 Allow the chromatogram to dry and then use a ruler to measure the distances that each of the visible pigments have travelled along the chromatography paper. Record your results. Some of the pigments may be very faint. Measure the distance to the centre of each of the pigment spots. When it is dry, stick the chromatogram in this workbook.

Results

Colour of extract in bright light:...

Distance moved by solvent (solvent front):..

Distances moved by each pigment:

pigment 1:..

pigment 2:..

pigment 3:..

pigment 4:..

pigment 5:..

Chromatogram:

Analysis, conclusion and evaluation

a   The **R_f value** for a pigment is a measure of how far it has travelled along the chromatogram, compared to the solvent. More soluble pigments will travel further and so have a higher R_f value. Different pigments will have a specific R_f value for a particular solvent.

Use the equation to calculate R_f values for each pigment and write them in Table 9.1.

R_f = distance moved by pigment ÷ distance moved by solvent

Pigment number on chromatogram	R_f value	Identity of pigment
1		
2		
3		
4		
5		

Table 9.1: Calculated results table.

b   Table 9.2. lists the known R_f values for several pigments, along with their colours. Use Table 9.2 and your calculated R_f values to identify each of the pigments. Record your answers in Table 9.1.

Pigment	R_f value in this solvent	Colour of spot
carotene	0.95	yellow
phaeophytin	0.83	yellow–grey
xanthophyll	0.71	yellow–brown
chlorophyll a	0.65	blue–green
chlorophyll b	0.45	green

Table 9.2: Known R_f values for pigments.

c   When placed into bright, focused light, the extract will change colour and fluoresce. This occurs because the pigments (especially chlorophyll) are absorbing light energy and then releasing it. If whole chloroplasts are used, fluorescence does not occur and light energy is not released. Explain why the pigment extract fluoresces but the whole chloroplasts do not.

....

....

KEY WORD

R_f value: a number that indicates how far a substance travels during chromatography, calculated by dividing the distance travelled by the substance by the distance travelled by the solvent; R_f values can be used to identify the substance

....

....

....

d i Explain why separating the pigments over a longer distance would not affect the R_f values.

....

....

ii Suggest why a longer distance would be used when there are more pigments present in the mixture.

....

....

....

....

e As the leaves of deciduous trees age, the number of pigments present changes and the leaves change colour, often turning red or golden. Outline a valid experiment that could be carried out to compare the different pigments and the quantity of chlorophyll pigment in leaves of different ages.

....

....

....

....

....

....

....

....

....

> **TIP**
>
> To reach a valid conclusion, you need to explain what variables need to be standardised and the method must generate reliable, accurate results. Colorimeters can also be used to assay quantities of pigment.

....

....

....

....

....

....

....

....

....

....

Practical Investigation 9.2: Effect of light intensity on the rate of photosynthesis

The rate of photosynthesis can be limited by several factors, including light intensity, light wavelength, temperature and carbon dioxide concentration. It is easy to measure the rate of photosynthesis by assaying the rate at which oxygen is produced by aquatic plants such as *Elodea* or *Cabomba*. In this experiment, you will observe the effect of changing light intensity on the rate of photosynthesis of an aquatic plant.

YOU WILL NEED

Equipment:
- glass microburette • 500 cm³, tall beaker • sodium hydrogencarbonate solution (1 mol dm⁻³), 50 cm³ • distilled water, 50 cm³ • scalpel • pondweed (*Elodea* or *Cabomba*) • syringe, 5 cm³ • screw clip • bench lamp • clamp, bosses (two of each) and stand • heatproof tile • paper clip • measuring cylinders, 10 cm³, 100 cm³ • one-metre ruler

Safety considerations

- Make sure you have read the Safety advice section at the beginning of this book and listen to any advice from your teacher before carrying out this investigation.

- Care should be taken with the burette as it is made of glass and breaks easily.

- Care should be taken with water around electric lamps and care should be taken to prevent cold water being splashed onto hot bulbs (this can cause the glass to break).

- Eye protection should be worn at all times.

- Scalpels are very sharp and should be handled carefully.

Method

1   Place 250 cm³ distilled water into the beaker.

2   Add 10 cm³ sodium hydrogencarbonate solution to the water.

3   Set up the equipment as shown in Figure 9.4. The stem of the pondweed should be cut at an approximately 45° angle to help oxygen release. One end of the pondweed should be undamaged. A paper clip should be placed on the undamaged end to weigh it down and the cut end placed so that it is inside the bulb of the microburette. The screw clip should be loosely attached to the rubber tubing at the top of the microburette.

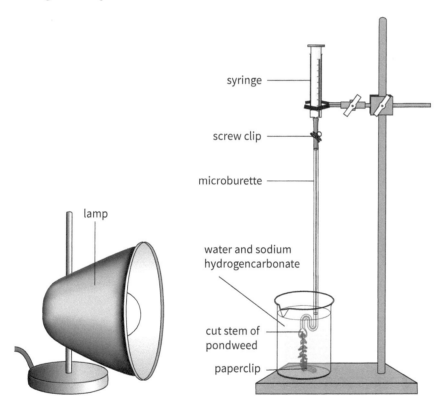

Figure 9.4: Apparatus for investigation 9.2.

4   Ensure that the pondweed and the bulb of the microburette are below the surface of the water and sodium hydrogencarbonate.

5   Use the syringe to draw up water into the bulb and part way up the microburette. Ensure that there is no air in the bulb or lower part of the tube and that the cut end of the pondweed is covered by water.

6   Place the meter ruler on the bench and place the bench lamp 135 mm away from the pondweed.

7   All main light sources in the room should be switched off and the bench lamp switched on. The pondweed should be lit for 5 min, or until a steady stream of gas production occurs. Check that bubbles are being released from the cut end of the stem – if they are not, try cutting the stem again with the scalpel and setting up the experiment again.

8   Use the syringe to draw up all the oxygen in the bulb and the stem of the microburette. Leave the pondweed to produce oxygen gas for 5 min, then draw up the gas into the stem of the capillary tube and measure the length of the oxygen bubble. If more than one bubble fills the stem, measure each and calculate the total length.

9   Repeat the procedure two more times with the lamp at the same distance from the pondweed (there is no need to leave the pondweed to adjust between readings). Record your results in Table 9.3.

10 Repeat the experiment with the lamp at distances of 148, 165, 191, 233 and 330 mm. Each time the distance of the lamp is moved, the pondweed should be left for 5 min to adjust to the new light intensity. Three readings should be obtained for each lamp distance. If the syringe is full of air, the clip should be screwed up, the syringe removed and the air expelled before replacing it. It may be necessary to add more water and sodium hydrogencarbonate in the beaker.

11 Measure and record the internal diameter (bore) of the burette.

Results

Distance of lamp from pondweed / mm	Light intensity / a.u.	Length of bubble produced in 5 min / mm			
		1	2	3	mean
135	6				
148	5				
165	4				
191	3				
233	2				
330	1				

Table 9.3: Results table.

Analysis, conclusion and evaluation

a   Calculate the mean bubble lengths for each light intensity. Do not include any values that appear anomalous. Record your answers in Table 9.3.

b   The bubble of oxygen in the stem of the burette is approximately the shape of a cylinder. Use the following formula for the volume of a cylinder to calculate the volume of oxygen produced and write your answers in Table 9.4.

$$V = \pi r^2 l$$

where:

r is the internal radius of the capillary tube (bore)

l is the total length of the bubble

c   Now, calculate the mean rate of oxygen production in $mm^3\ min^{-1}$ and record your answers in Table 9.4.

Distance of lamp from pondweed / mm	Light intensity / a.u.	Volume of oxygen produced in 5 min / mm³	Rate of oxygen production/ mm³ min⁻¹
135	6		
148	5		
165	4		
191	3		
233	2		
330	1		

Table 9.4: Calculated results table.

d   Plot an appropriate graph to show the effect of light intensity on the rate of oxygen production. Light intensity is inversely proportionate to the square of the distance of the lamp. The distances you used were selected to give relative light intensities with a range that is easy to plot on a graph.

e   Describe the pattern shown by your graph and results.

....

....

....

....

....

f   Use your knowledge of photosynthesis and limiting factors to explain the patterns
shown by your graph.

....

....

....

....

....

....

....

....

g   In Practical Investigation 8.2, you carried out a Spearman's rank correlation
coefficient test. Use the same statistical test to determine whether or not there is a
significant correlation between light intensity and rate of oxygen production.

h Explain why some sodium hydrogencarbonate was added to the water.

....

....

i Look carefully at your raw data. Identify any anomalous readings and suggest what could have caused them.

....

....

....

....

j Use the results of your statistical test and the reliability of the raw data to comment on the validity of your conclusion.

....

....

....

....

....

k Suggest two other variables that could have affected the results and give a method for standardising or monitoring them.

....

....

....

....

....

....

....

Practical Investigation 9.3: Gas exchange in a water plant

The basic equations for photosynthesis and aerobic respiration are the direct opposite of each other:

$$6\ CO_2 + 6\ H_2O \xrightleftharpoons[\text{respiration}]{\text{photosynthesis}} C_6H_{12}O_6 + 6\ O_2$$

Photosynthesis is affected by light intensity; respiration is not affected by light intensity and occurs in both the light and dark. In this practical, you will investigate how different conditions affect the gas exchange of pondweed.

Hydrogencarbonate indicator solution is a mixture of two pH indicators: thymol blue and cresol red. The indicator solution is in equilibrium with carbon dioxide in the environment. If there is an increase in carbon dioxide gas in the environment, more will dissolve in the indicator solution and form carbonic acid, lowering the pH.

Hydrogencarbonate indicator is red at a pH of 8.4 which is equivalent to an atmospheric carbon dioxide concentration of 0.04%. As the pH rises, the indicator solution changes to magenta and eventually purple. As the pH falls, the indicator changes to orange and eventually to yellow (shown in Figure 9.5.).

increasing CO_2 in indicator ←——————   atmospheric CO_2 level   decreasing CO_2 in indicator ——————→

yellow		orange		red		magenta		purple
pH 7.6	pH 7.8	pH 8.0	pH 8.2	pH 8.4	pH 8.6	pH 8.8	pH 9.0	pH 9.2

Figure 9.5: pH indicator range.

YOU WILL NEED

Equipment:
• five boiling tubes with rubber bungs • hydrogencarbonate indicator solution, 200 cm³ • four pieces of pondweed (*Elodea* or *Cabomba*) • bench lamp • aluminium foil • muslin cloth, three pieces • boiling-tube rack (or large glass beaker) • measuring cylinder, 20 or 50 cm³ • four rubber bands

Safety considerations

• Make sure you have read the Safety advice section at the beginning of this book and listen to any advice from your teacher before carrying out this investigation.

• Hydrogencarbonate indicator (thymol blue and cresol red) is listed as an irritant. If you splash on skin, wash with water. If splashed in your eye, wash your eye with running water.

• Eye protection should be worn.

Method

1 Label the boiling tubes 1–5. Cut four pieces of pondweed of similar size and place each into a boiling tube. Leave boiling tube 5 empty.

2 Add 20 cm³ hydrogencarbonate indicator to boiling tubes 1–4 and close each with a bung.

3 Totally cover boiling tube 1 with foil. The foil must prevent light entering from all areas.

4 Totally cover boiling tube 2 with one layer of the muslin cloth and secure it with rubber bands.

5 Totally cover boiling tube 3 with two layers of muslin cloth and secure them with rubber bands. Leave boiling tube 4 uncovered.

6 Place boiling tubes 1–4 into the boiling tube rack or glass beaker.

7 Fill boiling tube 5 with 20 cm³ hydrogencarbonate indicator but do not add any pondweed. Insert a rubber bung and place it in the boiling tube rack or glass beaker.

TIP

Bungs need to be secure to prevent entry and exit of gases.

8   Place the bench lamp 300 mm away from the boiling tubes and switch it on as shown in Figure 9.6.

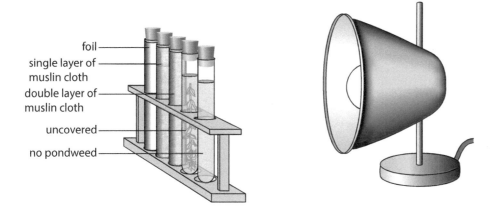

Figure 9.6: Apparatus for investigation 9.3.

9   After 1 h, remove the coverings and observe the colours of the indicator in each boiling tube and record them in Table 9.5.

Results

Boiling tube number	Conditions	Hydrogencarbonate indicator colour
1	foil	
2	one layer of muslin cloth	
3	two layers of muslin cloth	
4	no covering	
5	no pondweed or covering	

Table 9.5: Results table.

Analysis, conclusion and evaluation

a   Describe the effect of changing light intensity on the colour of the hydrogencarbonate indicator.

....

....

....

....

....

b Write a detailed explanation of your results. You will need to address the following points:

- what the hydrogencarbonate indicator shows about the pH changes

- why the pH changes in terms of net carbon dioxide release or use

- why the different light intensities cause changes in pH.

....

....

....

....

....

....

....

....

....

....

....

....

....

....

c Explain why the boiling tubes were sealed with rubber bungs.

....

....

d The results from this practical are qualitative rather than quantitative. Explain how this affects accuracy and suggest how the experiment could be altered to give quantitative results.

....

....

....

....

....

....

....

e   i In the 19th century, it was common practice to keep large numbers of plants during the day in hospital wards for people with breathing difficulties.

Explain why at night, when the lights were switched off, the plants were all removed from the ward.

....

....

....

....

ii Before winter, gardeners often place plants in greenhouses to prevent frost damage. The greenhouses are kept at a temperature of approximately 5 °C. Use your knowledge of limiting factors to explain why plants die when they are kept at temperatures of between 15 and 25 °C without artificial lighting in winter.

....

....

....

....

Practical Investigation 9.4: The effect of light wavelength on the light-dependent reaction (Hill reaction)

This Investigation, like Practical Investigation 8.3, uses redox indicators. Redox indicators such as 2,6-dichlorophenolindophenol (DCPIP) and methylene blue are often used to detect oxidation and reduction reactions. When both these substances accept electrons (or hydrogen), that is, are reduced, they change colour from blue to colourless as shown in Figure 9.7. Both are blue in their oxidised state. The light-dependent reaction in photosynthesis involves a series of redox reactions and so DCPIP can be used to monitor its rate.

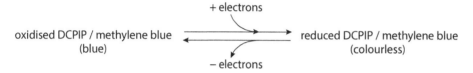

Figure 9.7: Colour change associated with oxidation / reduction of DCPIP.

In this practical, you will investigate the effect of changing the colour of light (wavelength) on the rate of the light-dependent reaction of isolated chloroplasts using DCPIP as an indicator.

> ### YOU WILL NEED
>
> **Equipment:**
> - spinach leaves (approximately ten) • measuring cylinder, 50 or 100 cm^3
> - muslin cloth • filter funnel • small beaker (labelled '1'), approximately 100 cm^3 • medium-size beaker (labelled '2'), approximately 250 cm^3 • large beaker (labelled '3'), approximately 500 cm^3 to use as an ice bath • ice
> - isolation medium, 100 cm^3 • DCPIP solution, 100 cm^3 • distilled water, 50 cm^3 • eight test tubes • eight test-tube bungs • test-tube rack
> - pipettes, 1 cm^3 and 10 cm^3 and fillers • bench lamp • glass marker pen
> - aluminium foil • coloured cellophane (light filters), purple, blue, green, orange and red
>
> **Access to:**
> - a blender • a sink

Safety considerations

- Make sure you have read the Safety advice section at the beginning of this book and listen to any advice from your teacher before carrying out this investigation.

- Eye protection should be worn at all times.

Method

It is essential that all glassware and substances are kept on ice as much as possible throughout the practical.

Part 1: Preparing the chloroplast extract

1 Half fill the large beaker (labelled '3') with ice and place beaker number '2' on the ice.

2 Remove the mid-rib from the spinach leaves and cut them up into small pieces using the scissors. Place the pieces into beaker number '2'.

3 Add approximately 50 cm³ cold isolation medium to the beaker and place the beaker back onto the ice.

4 Pour the contents of beaker '2' into the blender and blend for approximately 15 s. Quickly return the extract to beaker '2' and place the beaker back on ice.

5 Place three layers of muslin cloth in the filter funnel (you will need to fold it twice).

6 Place the small beaker (labelled number '1') on the ice.

7 Wet the muslin cloth with a small amount of ice cold isolation medium and then pour the chloroplast extract in beaker '2' into the muslin cloth. Filter the mixture into beaker '1' (as shown in Figure 9.8).

> **TIP**
>
> Fold and squeeze the muslin cloth to help the filtration.

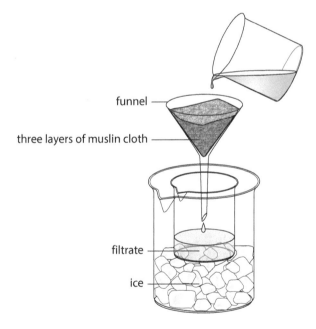

funnel —

three layers of muslin cloth —

filtrate —

ice —

Figure 9.8: Apparatus for part 1 of investigation 9.4.

8 The extract in beaker '1' should now be kept on the ice in beaker '3'.

Part 2: Comparing the effect of light wavelength on the time taken to decolourise DCPIP

1   Take eight test tubes and label them 1–8.

2   Use a pipette to place 5 cm³ DCPIP solution into tubes 1–7.

3   Use a pipette to place 5 cm³ distilled water into tube 8 (this tube is to act as a colour comparison to detect when DCPIP has decolourised).

4   Wrap aluminium foil around tube 7 so that it reaches the top of the tube. This tube will act as a control to show the effects of no light on DCPIP decolourisation.

5   Wrap different layers of coloured cellulose light filters around tubes 2–6 as listed in Table 9.6 in the Results section. The filters can be secured with adhesive tape and should reach the tops of the tubes (see Figure 9.9). The filter should not be too tight so that the tubes can be removed easily for examination and replaced into the coloured 'sleeve'.

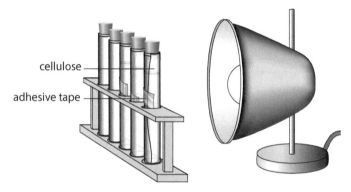

cellulose

adhesive tape

Figure 9.9: Apparatus for part 2 of investigation 9.4.

6   Place all eight test tubes into test-tube racks 10 cm from the bench lamp.

7   Use the pipette to add 1 cm³ chloroplast extract to each test tube, quickly mix each solution and place a bung in the top of each tube.

8   Switch on the lamp and check the colour of the solutions in tubes 1–6 every minute by removing the tube from its sleeve and then quickly replacing it. Do not remove the foil from test tube 7.

9   Record the times taken for the DCPIP to decolourise in each test tube to the nearest 60 s. You should compare them with the colour of tube 8 which has no DCPIP. If no colour change occurs after 15 min, record 'no change' in Table 9.6.

Results

Test-tube number	Colour of filter	Approximate light wavelength / nm	Time taken for DCPIP to decolourise / s
1	no filter	n/a	
2	purple	425	
3	blue	450	
4	green	525	
5	orange	625	
6	red	675	

Table 9.6: Results table.

Analysis, conclusion and evaluation

a **i** Record all the class results in Table 9.7. Circle any anomalies and calculate the mean times taken for DCPIP to decolourise for each filter.

Test-tube number	Colour of filter	Approximate light wavelength / nm	Times taken for DCPIP to decolourise / s	Mean time taken for DCPIP to decolourise / s	Mean rate of decolourisation of DCPIP / s^{-1}
1	no filter	n/a			
2	purple	425			
3	blue	450			
4	green	525			
5	orange	625			
6	red	675			

Table 9.7: Class results table.

ii Calculate the mean rates of decolourisation of DCPIP by using the equation:

$$rate = 1 \div time\ taken$$

Record the rates of decolourisation in Table 9.7.

b Plot an appropriate graph to show the effect of light colour or wavelength on the rate of decolourisation of DCPIP. You may choose either light colour or wavelength for the x-axis but your choice will affect the type of graph that you plot (bar chart or line graph).

c   Describe the patterns shown by your results and the class results.

....

....

....

....

....

....

d   Use your knowledge of photosynthesis and the absorption spectra to give a full explanation of the results. You should include:

•   the absorption and action spectra of the photosynthetic pigments

•   why DCPIP changes colour and how this links to the light-dependent reaction.

....

....

....

....

....

....

....

....

....

....

e   i   State the independent and dependent variables in this investigation:

independent variable:..

dependent variable:..

ii   Give **one** variable that was standardised and list variables that were not standardised but may have affected the results. Briefly suggest a method for standardising these variables.

standardised variable:...

variables that were not standardised:..

method for standardising the variables:

....

....

f   Comment on the reliability of the raw class data (consider the number of replicates and the similarity of the results).

....

....

....

g   Comment on the major limitations of the experiment and suggest methods for improvement.

....

....

....

h   The isolation medium is an ice-cold, isotonic buffer. Explain why it is:
   i   ice-cold

....

....

   ii   isotonic

....

....

Practical Investigation 9.5: The effect of carbon dioxide concentration on rate of photosynthesis

Light intensity, temperature and carbon dioxide concentration can all limit the rate of photosynthesis. In Practical Investigation 9.2, you will have investigated the effect of light intensity. In this practical, you will use a different method for investigating the effect of carbon dioxide concentration of the photosynthesis rate of plant tissue.

YOU WILL NEED

Equipment:

- 10 leaves (spinach or green cabbage leaves) • syringe, $10\,cm^3$ • cork borer or straw • sodium hydrogencarbonate solution ($1\,mol\,dm^{-3}$), $100\,cm^3$ • distilled water, $100\,cm^3$ • six small beakers, $50\,cm^3$ • modelling clay • bench lamp • timer

Safety considerations

- Make sure you have read the Safety advice section at the beginning of this book and listen to any advice from your teacher before carrying out this investigation.

- Eye protection should be worn.

Method

1   Use the cork borer or straw to cut 30 leaf discs. Do not take sections with mid-rib or thick veins.

2   Label the six beakers: 1.0, 0.8, 0.6, 0.4, 0.2, 0.0.

3   Calculate the volumes of $1\,mol\,dm^{-3}$ sodium hydrogencarbonate and distilled water that must be mixed to make up $10\,cm^3$ of each of the concentrations. Write your answers in Table 9.8.

Concentration of sodium hydrogen carbonate / $mol\,dm^{-3}$	Volume of $1\,mol\,dm^{-3}$ sodium hydrogen carbonate / cm^3	Volume of distilled water / cm^3
1.0		
0.8		
0.6		
0.4		
0.2		
0.0		

Table 9.8: Method preparation.

4   Make up the different concentrations of sodium hydrogencarbonate solutions in the appropriate beakers.

5   Remove the plunger from the syringe, put your finger over the nozzle to prevent it leaking, and fill it with 1.0 mol dm^{-3} sodium hydrogencarbonate.

6   Place five leaf discs into the solution in the syringe.

7   Carefully replace the plunger and turn the syringe so the nozzle is pointing upwards. Let out any air by pushing down the plunger.

8   When no air is present in the syringe, place a finger tightly over the nozzle and pull the plunger down. Bubbles will appear on the leaves. Tap the syringe to move the bubbles and let out the gas from the nozzle. Repeat until all the discs have sunk to the base of the syringe.

9   Place a piece of modelling clay on the bench (see Figure 9.10) and fix the plunger of the syringe in it so that the nozzle is pointing upwards. Place the bench lamp so that it is 10 cm away from the syringe.

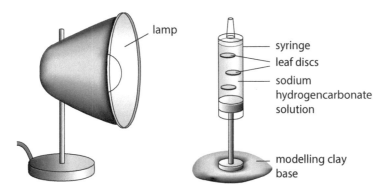

Figure 9.10: Apparatus for investigation 9.5.

10 Start the timer and record the time taken for each disc to float to the top of the solution in Table 9.9.

11 Repeat for each concentration of sodium hydrogencarbonate.

Results

Concentration of sodium hydrogencarbonate / mol dm^{-3}	Time taken for discs to float to surface / s					
	1	2	3	4	5	mean
1.0						
0.8						
0.6						
0.4						
0.2						
0.0						

Table 9.9: Results table.

Analysis, conclusion and evaluation

a **i** Calculate the mean times taken for the discs to float to the surface and record them in Table 9.9.

    ii Draw an appropriate graph to present your results.

b Describe the pattern shown by your graph.

....

....

....

c Explain why the leaf discs float to the surface when lit.

....

....

d Use your knowledge of photosynthesis and limiting factors to explain your results.

....

....

....

e **i** State **two** variables that were standardised.

1 ....

2 ....

ii Suggest **one** variable that was not standardised, and would affect the result. Suggest a method that could be used to standardise it.

variable: ....

method: ....

f Look carefully at the replicates that you carried out. The mean times for different concentrations of sodium hydrogencarbonate may be different but there may be 'overlaps' of raw data. For example, the first disc to float in distilled water may have taken 321 s and the last disc to float in a concentration of $0.2 \, mol \, dm^{-3}$ might also have taken 321 s or more. Comment on the reliability of your conclusion after taking into account the raw data.

....

....

....

g   Outline a further experiment that could be carried out to determine whether
    temperature was also acting as a limiting factor for photosynthesis.

    ....

    ....

    ....

    ....

    ....

Chapter 10

Homeostasis and coordination

This chapter relates to Chapter 14: Homeostasis and Chapter 15: Control and coordination, in the Coursebook.

In this chapter, you will complete practical investigations on:

- 10.1 The structure of the kidney

- 10.2 Analysis of urine

- 10.3 The role of gibberellic acid in the germination of barley seeds

- 10.4 The effect of light wavelength on phototropism in wheat seedlings

- 10.5 Investigating human reflexes

Practical Investigation 10.1:
The structure of the kidney

This practical should help to give you an understanding of the internal structure of the mammalian kidney. One of the most important skills of biology is making the link between structure and function. The dissection of the kidney is a very good example of how organs are designed to carry out particular functions, in this case, excretion and osmoregulation.

YOU WILL NEED

Equipment:
• one fresh lamb's kidney • scalpel • forceps • mounted needle • tray (to keep the kidney in during the dissection) • hydrogen peroxide, 20 Volume, in a dropper bottle • prepared microscope slides of kidney

Access to:
• sink • running water • hand-washing facilities • gloves if requested • sterilising fluid and cloths

Safety considerations

- Make sure you have read the Safety advice section at the beginning of this book and listen to any advice from your teacher before carrying out this investigation.

- Wash hands with soap and water after handling the kidney. Wipe down all surfaces with disinfectant after the practical.

- Hydrogen peroxide is classed as corrosive and an irritant, particularly to the eyes. Eye protection should be worn at all times. If you splash on skin, wash with water.

- Scalpels, forceps and mounted needles should be handled with care as they can easily cause cuts.

Method

Part 1: Kidney dissection

1 Take a kidney and place it in a tray. If it is covered in solid fat, carefully remove the fat whilst trying to keep the ureter and blood vessels complete.

2 Lay the kidney on its side as shown in Figure 10.1. Try to locate the ureter, renal artery and renal vein.

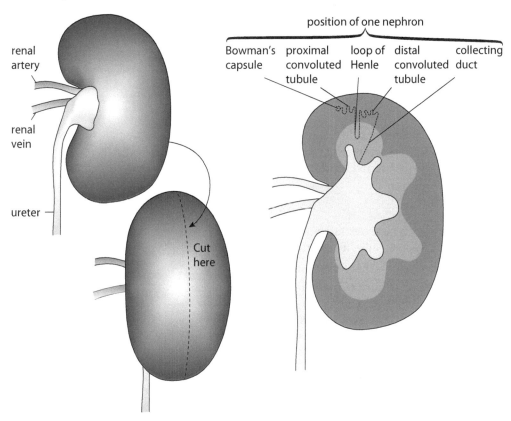

Figure 10.1: External and internal structures of a kidney.

3 Cut the kidney open by making a longitudinal cut opposite the ureter and blood vessels. Cut the kidney into two halves and separate them. Identify the following features (shown in Figure 10.1):

- cortex – the brown outer region; tiny specks of red (the glomeruli) may be visible

- medulla – the red middle region that fades to a white colour in the centre

- pelvis – the inner, yellow coloured section

- ureter – thick tube that will be attached to the pelvis

- renal artery and vein – the two blood vessels that will be close to the ureter.

4   Draw a diagram of the kidney in the space provided labelling all the visible features.

5   Use the dropping pipette to pour some hydrogen peroxide over the cortex and medulla. This will foam vigorously. Carefully scrape off the foam; you may now be able to identify collecting ducts, loops of Henle and renal tubules where bubbles have formed inside the tubules.

Part 2: Ultrastructure of the kidney

6   Tidy away the kidney and set up a microscope. Look at a prepared section (TS) of a kidney. Try to distinguish cortex from medulla. The cortex should have glomeruli present which are absent in the medulla.

7   Switch to high power and focus on a region of cortex. Try to identify glomeruli, Bowman's capsule, and cross-sections through renal tubules. It may be possible to distinguish between the proximal and distal convoluted tubules (use Figure 10.2, which shows the ultrastructure of kidney cortex showing glomeruli, Bowman's capsule, proximal and distal convoluted tubules, to help you identify the structures).

TIP
Proximal convoluted tubule cells have a brush border of microvilli on the inside of the tubule which is absent on the distal convoluted tubule cells. There is a slightly narrower lumen.
Distal convoluted tubules do not have a brush border and tend to have a wider lumen.

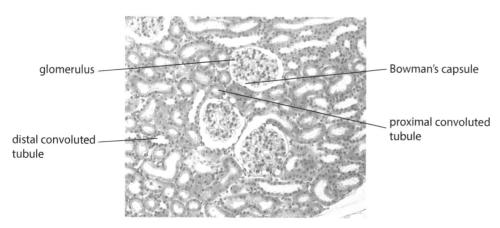

Figure 10.2: Photomicrograph of transverse section of kidney cortex.

8   Draw a plan diagram showing some of the tubules in different planes, label some glomeruli, renal tubules (proximal and distal if possible) and Bowman's capsules.

9   Focus on a section of medulla and try to identify collecting ducts, the thick and thin limbs of the loop of Henle and the capillaries of the vasa recta.

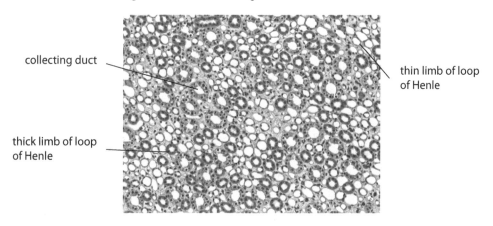

Figure 10.3: Photomicrograph of transverse section of kidney medulla.

10 Draw a diagram labelling as many of these structures as you can identify (use Figure 10.3, which shows a section through the medulla of a kidney showing collecting ducts and thick and thin limbs of loop of Henle, to help you).

- collecting ducts

- thick limbs of the loop of Henle

- thin limbs of the loop of Henle

- vasa recta capillaries.

- Collecting ducts are the widest diameter tubules with thick columnar epithelial cells.

- Thick limbs of the loop of Henle will have a wide diameter (although smaller than the collecting ducts) with thick cuboidal epithelial cells.

- Thin limbs of the loop of Henle will have a narrow diameter and a thin layer of flattened epithelial cells.

- Vasa recta capillaries are difficult to distinguish from the thin limbs of the loop of Henle. They are narrow with a thin endothelium, a slightly less regular shape and may have blood cells inside them.

Analysis, conclusion and evaluation

a   Use your results and your own knowledge to explain how the structure of each
    area of the nephron is adapted to its function by completing Table 10.1.

Area of nephron	Structural features	Function
glomerulus and Bowman's capsule		
proximal convoluted tubule		
distal convoluted tubule		
loop of Henle		
collecting duct		

Table 10.1: Nephron features and functions.

b   Explain why some of the tubules appear circular but some appear cylindrical.

    ....

    ....

c   In Chapter 3, you carried out a practical with the enzyme urease. Plan an investigation into how you could use urease enzyme to observe the effect of protein in the diet on the concentration of urea found in human urine. You should include the following:

- hypothesis

- method for measuring the dependent variable with practical details

- how you will ensure reliability

- what factors you will standardise and how you will standardise them.

....

....

....

....

....

....

....

....

....

....

....

....

....

....

....

....

....

....

....

....

....

....

Practical Investigation 10.2: Analysis of urine

The composition of urine can be a good indicator of the health or physiological state of an individual. For example, diabetics often have very high concentrations of blood glucose. One method used to diagnose diabetes is the detection of glucose in the urine. Patients with high blood pressure also often have protein present in their urine due to excessive filtration pressure.

In this practical you will carry out a series of biochemical tests on different samples of urine to diagnose the conditions that they may indicate.

YOU WILL NEED

Equipment:
- large beaker, $500\,cm^3$ • 16 test tubes • Bunsen burner, tripod and gauze (or hot water bath) • biuret solution, $30\,cm^3$ • Benedict's solution, $30\,cm^3$ • four conical flasks, $250\,cm^3$ • syringe, $5\,cm^3$ or $2\,cm^3$ • silver nitrate solution, $0.1\,mol\,dm^{-3}$, $50\,cm^3$ • potassium thiocyanate, $0.1\,mol\,dm^{-3}$, $100\,cm^3$ • saturated iron (III) nitrate solution in a dropper bottle, $10\,cm^3$ • timer • four samples of urine, labelled A, B, C and D; $20\,cm^3$ of each in labelled beakers • pipette, $10\,cm^3$

Safety considerations

- Make sure you have read the Safety advice section at the beginning of this book and listen to any advice from your teacher before carrying out this investigation.

- Potassium thiocyanate is classed as harmful by ingestion and should not be heated.

- Silver nitrate solution and saturated iron (III) nitrate are harmful in contact with skin, on ingestion and are oxidising agents.

- Eye protection should be worn and all splashes and spills washed off with water.

Method

Part 1: Benedict's test

1   Label four test tubes A, B, C and D.

2   Use a pipette to place $5\,cm^3$ of each of the samples of urine (A, B, C and D) into the appropriate test tubes.

3   Set up an $80\,°C$ water bath using the $500\,cm^3$ beaker and Bunsen burner, tripods and gauze or hot water from a kettle.

4   Add $5\,cm^3$ Benedict's solution to each test tube.

5   Place the test tubes into the hot water bath and leave for 10 min.

6   Record the colours of the solutions in Table 10.2.

Part 2: Biuret test

7   Label four test tubes A, B, C and D.

8   Use a pipette to place $5\,cm^3$ of each of the samples of urine (A, B, C and D) into the appropriate test tubes.

9   Add $5\,cm^3$ biuret reagent to each test tube.

10   Mix the solutions and record the colours of the solutions in Table 10.2.

Part 3: Sodium chloride test

11   Label the conical flasks A, B, C and D.

12   Place $2\,cm^3$ urine in the appropriate flask.

13   Add $10\,cm^3$ $0.1\,mol\,dm^{-3}$ silver nitrate solution into each conical flask and mix. The urine should go cloudy as chloride ions are precipitated as white silver chloride. Leave the mixture for between 5 and 10 min.

14   Add five drops of a saturated solution of iron (lll) nitrate to the solutions in the conical flasks. This is an indicator solution for excess potassium thiocyanate.

15   Fill the syringe with $0.1\,mol\,dm^3$ potassium thiocyanate. Carefully add $0.1\,mol\,dm^3$ potassium thiocyanate from the syringe into conical flask 'A', stirring the flask all the time (see Figure 10.4). Stop when a red colour appears and remains for at least 15 s. You may need to refill the syringe. Record the total volume of thiocyanate required in Table 10.2. Repeat this with the other samples of urine in flasks B, C and D.

Figure 10.4: Technique for method of part 3 of investigation 10.2.

Results

Urine sample	Colour of Benedict's solution	Colour of biuret reagent	Volume of potassium thiocyanate added / cm³
A			
B			
C			
D			

Table 10.2: Results table.

Analysis, conclusion and evaluation

Determining the salt concentration of the urine samples

The method that you have used to determine the concentration of sodium chloride ions in the urine samples is known as a *back titration*.

The urine samples all contain sodium chloride in solution (NaCl).

When dissolved in water, NaCl dissociates into Na^+ and Cl^- ions:

$$NaCl(s) \rightarrow Na^+(aq) + Cl^-(aq)$$

When silver nitrate solution was added, the silver ions reacted with the chloride ions to form an insoluble precipitate of silver chloride:

$$AgNO_3 + NaCl \rightarrow AgCl \text{ (solid precipitate)} + NaNO_3$$

This reduced the concentration of chloride ions and silver ions in the solution. The higher the concentration of salt (chloride ions) in the urine, the more silver ions removed. Silver nitrate was added in excess so that when the precipitation was completed, there was no chloride in solution. The concentration of silver ions left depends on how much chloride was present – high concentration of chloride ions will reduce the silver ion concentration by more than a low concentration of chloride ions.

The iron indicator (Fe^{3+}) was added and the solution was titrated with the potassium thiocyanate solution. The potassium thiocyanate reacts with unprecipitated silver nitrate:

$$KCNS + AgNO_3 \rightarrow KNO_3 + AgCNS$$

As soon as all the silver nitrate solution has been used up, the potassium thiocyanate reacts with the iron (III) nitrate indicator, forming red iron (lll) thiocyanate.

a   The mass (g) of chloride ions in $2\,cm^3$ urine may be calculated by using the formula:

$$(10 - x) \times \left(\frac{35.5}{10}\right) \times \left(\frac{1}{1000}\right)$$

where x is the volume of potassium thiocyanate added.

 i   Calculate the mass in grams of chloride ions present in each $2\,cm^3$ of each urine sample and record your values in Table 10.3.

 ii   Convert the mass of chlorides found in $2\,cm^3$ urine into the concentration of urine in $g\,cm^{-3}$. Record your results in Table 10.3.

Urine sample	Volume of potassium thiocyanate added (x) / cm³	Mass of chloride in 2 cm³ urine / g	Concentration of chloride ions in urine / g cm⁻³
A			
B			
C			
D			

Table 10.3: Results table.

b Summarise your findings from the Benedict's tests, biuret tests and salt concentrations in Table 10.4.

Urine sample	Presence / absence of glucose	Presence / absence of protein	Concentration of chloride ions in urine / $g\,cm^{-3}$
A			
B			
C			
D			

Table 10.4: Results table.

c You were presented with four different samples of urine:

- one from a person who has too much dietary salt

- one from a person with type 1 diabetes

- one from a person with high blood pressure

- a control sample from a person with no known conditions and a normal diet.

Identify each of the urine samples, and in each case, use your knowledge to give a detailed explanation of the reasons for the composition of the urine.

i too much dietary salt

....

....

....

....

ii Type 1 diabetes

....

....

....

....

iii   high blood pressure

....

....

....

....

iv   no known conditions and a normal diet.

....

....

....

....

d   i   State which of the tests give qualitative or quantitative results.

....

....

ii   Suggest how the practical could be adapted so all the tests give quantitative results.

....

....

Practical Investigation 10.3: The role of gibberellic acid in the germination of barley seeds

Seeds contain insoluble storage compounds such as starch in the endosperm tissue. When seeds begin to germinate, the embryo releases gibberellic acid which stimulates the aleurone layer of the seed to produce the enzyme amylase. This now begins to hydrolyse starch into soluble maltose which can be absorbed and metabolised by the embryo. This practical investigates the effect of different concentrations of gibberellic acid on the activation of amylase in barley seeds. The activity of amylase will be assayed by using a starch agar plate.

YOU WILL NEED

Equipment:

• six starch agar plates each containing a different concentration of gibberellic acid • razor blade or scalpel • marker pen • barley seeds (40) that have been soaked in water for between 6 and 8 h • 3% sodium hypochlorite solution (bleach) • forceps • tea strainer or sieve • iodine solution • pipettes, 1 cm^3 and 10 cm^3 and fillers • three beakers, 50 cm^3 • small, sterile bottles or containers with lids • tile for cutting on • adhesive tape • distilled water, 100 cm^3

Access to:

• incubator (or warm place) at a temperature of between 20 and 30 °C

Safety considerations

- Make sure you have read the Safety advice section at the beginning of this book and listen to any advice from your teacher before carrying out this investigation.

- Sodium hypochlorite solution is an irritant.

- Iodine solution is an irritant and a possible environmental hazard so should not be thrown away near natural water.

- Gibberellic acid is classed as low risk but may cause minor irritation.

- Razor blades and scalpels should be handled with care.

- Eye protection should always be worn. If you splash on skin, wash with water.

- After incubation, the starch agar plate should not be re-opened and will need to be thrown away safely as it could represent a biohazard.

Method

1   Look carefully at the barley seeds and use Figure 10.5 to identify the half which contains the endosperm and the half with the embryo.

2   Half fill a small beaker with 3% sodium hypochlorite solution.

3   Using the razor blade or scalpel on the tile, carefully cut 30 barley seeds in half using a transverse cut (as shown in Figure 10.5). Discard the halves containing the embryo and place the endosperm halves into the 3% sodium hypochlorite solution. Leave them for approximately 5 min.

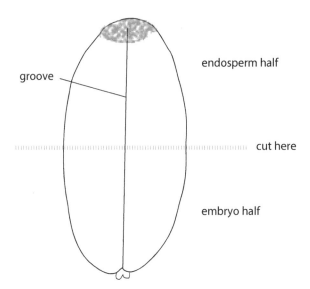

Figure 10.5: Method for making a transverse cut for investigation 10.3.

4   Take a starch agar plate for each concentration of gibberellic acid ($1 \times 10^{-20}\%$, $1 \times 10^{-30}\%$, $1 \times 10^{-40}\%$, $1 \times 10^{-50}\%$, $1 \times 10^{-60}\%$, 0%)

5   Place the tea strainer or sieve over a beaker and strain the pieces of seed. Wash repeatedly (five or six times) with sterile distilled water so that the seeds no longer smell of the sodium hypochlorite solution.

6   Using the forceps, evenly place five of the pieces of seed onto each of the agar plates. Position them so that the cut-side is touching the agar and they are in an approximate circle as shown in Figure 10.6.

7   Secure the lids of the starch agar plates with some adhesive tape and place them in a warm incubator (between 20 and 30 °C) for 36 h.

8   After 36 h, open the Petri dishes slightly (do not remove the lid fully as pathogens may have grown on the agar) and flood the plates with iodine solution.

9   If the aleurone has been activated by the gibberellic acid, amylase should have been produced and it will have diffused into the agar, digesting the starch. This will be shown by the presence of areas around the seed which do not stain blue–black with iodine solution (as shown in Figure 10.6). The higher the amylase concentration, the wider the area. Use a ruler to measure the maximum widths of the clear circles and record your results in Table 10.5 in the Results section.

Figure 10.6: Effect of amylase on starch.

Results

Concentration of gibberellic acid / %	Diameter of clear zone around each seed / mm					
	1	2	3	4	5	mean
0						
1×10^{-6}						
1×10^{-5}						
1×10^{-4}						
1×10^{-3}						
1×10^{-2}						

Table 10.5: Results table.

Analysis, conclusion and evaluation

a Calculate the mean diameters of the clear zones for each concentration of gibberellic acid. Record your answers in Table 10.5.

b Plot a bar chart to show the effect of concentration of gibberellic acid on the mean diameter of the clear zone.

c Describe the patterns shown by your graph.

....

....

....

d To decide on how strong our conclusion is, we can add **error bars** to the points on the graph. The error bars show us the range about the mean within which we would expect, with 95% confidence, that values would lie if we repeated the experiment again. To draw error bars, we need to calculate the **standard deviation** of the data and the **standard error**.

Standard deviation

Calculate the standard deviation of the clear zone diameter for a concentration of 1×10^{-2} using the following steps:

i Write the results for each of the repeats (x) at 1×10^{-2} in column (I) of Table 10.6.

ii Subtract the mean from each of the repeats using the equation:

$$(x - \bar{x})$$

where:

x = value of the repeat

$\bar{x}$ = mean

and write your calculated values in column (II)

iii Calculate the square of each $(x - \bar{x})$ term and write your calculated values in column (III)

Repeat number	(I) Diameter of clear zone around each seed (x) / mm	(II) $(x - \bar{x})$	(III) $(x - \bar{x})^2$
1			
2			
3			
4			
5			
			$\Sigma(x - \bar{x})^2 =$

Table 10.6: Calculated results table.

iv Calculate $\Sigma(x - \bar{x})^2$. This equation means 'the sum of all the $(x - \bar{x})^2$ terms'. You just need to add up all the of the numbers in column (III). Write your answer in Table 10.6.

KEY WORDS

error bars: there is a 95% certainty that the true mean lies within the range of an error bar that extends two standard errors above the mean and two standard errors below the mean

standard deviation: a measure of how widely a set of data is spread out on either side of the mean

standard error: a measure of how likely it is that a mean calculated from a sample represents the true mean for the whole population

v   Now, use the equation for standard deviation to calculate the standard deviation:

$$\sigma = \sqrt{\frac{\Sigma(x - \bar{x})^2}{n - 1}}$$

where:

σ = standard deviation

n = number of repeats

$\Sigma(x - \bar{x})^2$ = sum of $(x - \bar{x})^2$ terms

$\sigma =$ ....

> **TIP**
>
> You can use your calculator to calculate standard deviations.

vi   Now, use the same method to calculate the standard deviation for the diameter of the clear zone at each concentration of gibberellic acid. Write your values in Table 10.7.

Concentration of gibberellic acid / %	Mean diameter of clear zone /mm	Standard deviation	Standard error	2 × standard error	95% confidence limits (lowest → highest)
0					
1×10^{-6}					
1×10^{-5}					
1×10^{-4}					
1×10^{-3}					
1×10^{-2}					

Table 10.7: Calculated results table.

Standard error and 95% confidence limits

e   i   Calculate the standard error for the mean diameter of the clear zone at each concentration of gibberellic acid using the formula:

$$SE = \frac{\sigma}{\sqrt{n}}$$

where:

SE is the standard error

σ is the standard deviation

n is the number of repeats

Write your values in Table 10.7.

ii   Calculate 2 × the standard error for the mean diameter of the clear zone at each concentration of gibberellic acid and write your values in Table 10.7.

iii   If we were to repeat the experiment, we can say with 95% confidence that the results would lie between the mean value ± 2 standard errors. We can calculate the range by determining the lowest and highest values of the confidence limits by determining:

lowest value = mean $(\bar{x})$ – 2 × standard error

highest value = mean $(\bar{x})$ + 2 × standard error

Calculate the confidence limits for the mean diameter of the clear zone at each concentration of gibberellic acid and write your values in Table 10.7.

f   Now that you have the **95% confidence limits**, you can plot them as error bars on your graph. Draw error bars about each of the plotted mean values like Figure 10.7.

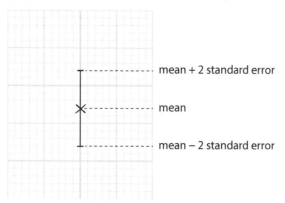

KEY WORD

95% confidence limits: a measure of how accurate a mean value is. There is a 95% probability that the true mean lies between ±2 standard errors of the mean

mean + 2 standard error

mean

mean − 2 standard error

Figure 10.7: Method for plotting error bars.

Error bars give us an indication of whether our mean values are significantly different. If there is no overlap between error bars around different mean values, we can be 95% certain that there is a statistical significant difference and that strengthens the evidence that there is a difference. If there is an overlap, the means may be different but the difference is not significantly different.

g   Use the error bars and confidence limits to discuss if there is strong evidence for the different concentrations of gibberellic acid resulting in different diameters of clear zones.

....

....

....

....

....

h   Use your knowledge to give a detailed explanation of the results.

....

....

....

....

....

....

i   Identify any anomalous values in your raw data and suggest reasons for them.

....

....

....

....

Practical Investigation 10.4: The effect of light wavelength on phototropism in wheat seedlings

Phototropism is the direction growth response of plants. Plant shoots will usually grow in the direction of the light due to the redistribution of the plant growth regulator auxin (IAA) in response to the direction of the light. The shoot tip must contain some form of photoreceptor that responds to light. The aim of this practical is to investigate which light wavelengths are detected by the photoreceptor.

YOU WILL NEED

Equipment:
- five shoe boxes with a 'window' cut out of the front (these may be shared between several groups) • five Petri dishes containing wheat seedlings
- bench lamps • ruler, 30 cm • cellophane light filters; red, blue, green, clear
- small piece of black card to fit over the window of one box

---

Safety considerations

- Make sure you have read the Safety advice section at the beginning of this book and listen to any advice from your teacher before carrying out this investigation.

- Make sure you do not have any allergies to plants and seeds.

Method

1   Take the shoe boxes and using the adhesive tape, attach a different coloured cellophane filter over the 'window' at the front. One box should have a clear cellophane 'window' that allows all light wavelengths through and one should have a piece of black card so that no light will enter (see Figure 10.8).

2   Take a Petri dish containing wheat coleoptiles. Using a pair of forceps, carefully remove any seedlings that have fallen over, have coleoptiles less than 10 mm in length or longer than 50 mm in length or have coleoptiles that do not seem to be growing correctly.

> **TIP**
>
> Some plants, such as wheat, have a protective sheath that covers the shoot. This sheath is a coleoptile.

3   Measure the lengths of the remaining coleoptiles and record them in Table 10.8 in the Results section.

4   Add some water to the cotton wool so that the seedlings do not dry out and place the Petri dish inside the shoe box with a clear filter. Place the box about 30 cm away from a light source such as a bench lamp, as shown in Figure 10.8. Repeat this for all the other shoe boxes with different light filters.

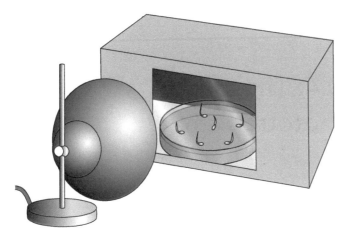

Figure 10.8: Apparatus for investigation 10.4.

5   After 24–48 h, inspect the wheat seedlings. Measure the lengths of the coleoptiles and count how many are bending towards the direction of the light source. Record the results in Tables 10.8–10.10. You will also need to record how many wheat seedlings were in each Petri dish. Make a descriptive comment in each case about the degree of curvature of the coleoptiles. If possible take a photograph and stick it into your notes.

Results

Starting length of coleoptile for each light colour / mm					
	No light (card)	Clear	Red	Green	Blue
mean					

Table 10.8: Results table: starting length.

Final length of coleoptile for each light colour / mm					
	No light (card)	Clear	Red	Green	Blue
mean					

Table 10.9: Results table: final length.

Light colour	Number of coleoptiles that grow towards light source	Total number of coleoptiles	Percentage of coleoptiles that grow towards light source	Observations on curvature
no light (card)				
clear				
red				
green				
blue				

Table 10.10: Combined results table.

Photograph:

Analysis, conclusion and evaluation

a Calculate the mean lengths of the coleoptiles at the start of the practical and after 24 h. Record the values in Tables 10.8 and 10.9.

b Calculate the percentage of coleoptiles that are growing in the direction of the light for each light colour. Record your calculations in Table 10.10.

c Calculate the changes in mean coleoptile length and record them in Table 10.11.

Light colour	Change in mean length of coleoptiles / mm
no light (card)	
clear	
red	
green	
blue	

Table 10.11: Calculated results table.

d Draw appropriate graphs on the grid that follows, to show your findings.

e Describe the effects of changing light colour on the growth of the coleoptiles.

....

....

....

....

....

....

f   Explain what the results show about the sensitivity of the wheat seedlings to different colours of light. Comment on the effect of light colour on the length of the coleoptiles and the curvature.

....

....

....

....

....

....

....

g   Suggest **two** variables that were not standardised in the experiment.

....

....

h   Comment on the strength of your conclusion (when considering your data). Suggest limitations with the method of analysis used.

....

....

....

i   Suggest how the analysis could be improved to investigate if the changes in length and number of seedlings that grow in the direction of light were statistically significant.

....

....

....

....

....

....

....

Practical Investigation 10.5: Investigating human reflexes

The nervous system plays a very important role in animal coordination. This investigation on reflexes compares the reaction times when responding to sight, touch and sound.

YOU WILL NEED

Equipment:
- 1 metre ruler
- A partner

Safety considerations

- Make sure you have read the Safety advice section at the beginning of this book and listen to any advice from your teacher before carrying out this investigation.

Method

1   The person being experimented upon (the subject) needs to sit down and place their forearm flat on a bench or table with their hand over the edge of the table (as shown in Figure 10.9).

2   The first finger and thumb are kept 3 cm apart and the end of the ruler is positioned between them with the end level with the bottom of the thumb.

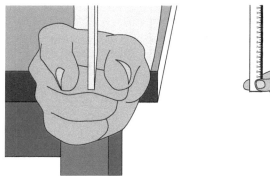 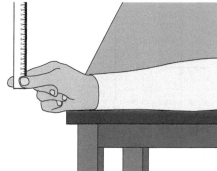

Figure 10.9: Method for investigation 10.5.

3   Without giving any clue, the ruler is dropped vertically and the subject must catch the ruler as soon as they see it move. Measure the distance the ruler has fallen to the bottom of the thumb. Repeat this to get ten readings. Record your results in Table 10.12.

4   The experiment is repeated but using touch as the sense that detects the ruler falling. The subject is blindfolded and the ruler is positioned between the thumb and first finger so that it just touches the first finger. Record your results in Table 10.12.

> **TIP**
>
> When investigating touch, make sure the ruler is touching the first finger otherwise the investigation will be about extra sensory perception!

5 The experiment is repeated a final time but this time using hearing as the sense that detects the ruler falling. The subject is blindfolded and the ruler is positioned between the thumb and first finger without touching. When the ruler is dropped, the experimenter calls 'Go!' and the subject catches the ruler as soon as they hear this. Record your results in Table 10.12.

Results

| Ruler drop number | Distances ruler fell and reaction times for different senses | | | | | |
| | Sight | | Touch | | Sound | |
	distance / cm	reaction time / s	distance / cm	reaction time / s	distance / cm	reaction time / s
1						
2						
3						
4						
5						
6						
7						
8						
9						
10						
Mean						
Standard deviation						

Table 10.12: Results table.

Analysis, conclusion and evaluation

a   You are first going to determine the actual reaction times for each reflex.

   i   Firstly, calculate the time taken (to three decimal places) for each of the readings in Table 10.12 to catch the ruler by using the formula:

$$t = \sqrt{\frac{d}{4.9}}$$

   The equation you used to determine the time taken is derived by rearranging the equation of motion:

$$d = \frac{1}{2}at^2$$

   where:

   d is the distance the ruler fell

   a is the acceleration due to gravity ($9.8\,\mathrm{m\,s^{-2}}$)

   t is the time taken

   ii   Calculate the mean distances the ruler fell and the mean reaction times for each experiment. Record your values in Table 10.12.

   iii   Calculate the standard deviations for the reaction times and write your answers in Table 10.12. Look back at Practical Investigation 10.3 if you are unsure how to calculate the standard deviations.

b   You have now found the reaction times. We can also use this to calculate the speed of transmission of the nerve impulse along the pathways.

   •   Sight: eye → brain → down spine to shoulders → along arm to forearm

   •   Touch: skin on finger → along arm to spine → up spine to brain → down spine to shoulder → along arm to forearm

   •   Sound: ear → brain → down spine to shoulders → along arm to forearm

   i   Measure the distances the impulses travel for the different reflexes. You will need to think about where the impulse starts (receptor), where it reaches the central nervous system (CNS) and where the effector is. Discuss this with other members of your class and your teacher. When you have measured the distances, record them in Table 10.13. Also record the mean reaction times.

Reflex type	Distance travelled by impulse / cm	Mean reaction time / cm	Impulse transmission speed / cm s⁻¹
sight			
touch			
sound			

Table 10.13: Results table.

   ii The transmission speed of the impulse is calculated by using the formula:

   transmission speed = distance travelled by impulse ÷ mean reaction time

   Calculate the transmission speeds for each of the reflex types and record your results in Table 10.13.

c Compare the reaction times and the speeds of transmission for the three reflex types giving explanations for the differences. Consider the lengths of the pathways and the effect of synapse number.

....

....

....

....

....

....

....

....

....

....

....

d Even though the mean reaction times of the different reflexes may be different it does not mean that they are significantly different. We can use the *t*-test to determine whether there are statistically significant differences.

   i In the first test, you will compare the reaction time for sight with the reaction time for touch. To start with, you need to formulate a null hypothesis. A null hypothesis states that there is no difference between the two factors you are comparing. Complete the null hypothesis to compare the reaction times:

   'There is no difference between...'

   ....

   ....

> KEY WORD

t-test: a statistical procedure used to determine whether the means of two samples differ significantly

ii   The formula for the *t*-test is:

$$t = \frac{|\bar{x}_1 - \bar{x}_2|}{\sqrt{\left(\dfrac{s_1^2}{n_1} + \dfrac{s_2^2}{n_2}\right)}}$$

where:

$\bar{x}_1$ is the mean of sample 1 (sight)

$\bar{x}_2$ is the mean of sample 2 (touch)

s_1 is the standard deviation of sample 1 (sight)

s_2 is the standard deviation of sample 2 (touch)

n_1 is the number of repeats in sample 1 (sight)

n_2 is the number of repeats in sample 2 (touch)

Use the formula and the results in Table 10.13 to calculate the *t*-value for comparing the sight and touch reflexes.

> **TIP**
>
> The straight-line brackets, $|\bar{x}_1 - \bar{x}_2|$, means 'absolute value' so we ignore any negative sign if the difference in means is negative.

$t = $ ....

iii   Now, calculate the number of degrees of freedom for all the data using the formula:

$$v = (n_1 - 1) + (n_2 - 1)$$

Degrees of freedom = ...

iv   Now you can use your calculated *t*-value and the degrees of freedom to see if there is a significant difference between the reaction times for sight and touch by looking up the critical value in a *t*-test table (Table 10.14). Look along the line for the calculated number of degrees of freedom and identify which of the critical values your calculated *t*-value is greater than. We can take a probability of 0.05 or less of the difference being due to chance as being the critical one which represents a statistically significant difference. For example, if the *t*-value is greater than 2.20 with 11 degrees of freedom, there is a probability of less than 0.05 that the difference is due to chance.

Degrees of freedom	Value of t			
1	6.31	12.7	63.7	63.6
2	2.92	4.30	9.93	31.6
3	2.35	3.18	5.84	12.9
4	2.13	2.78	4.60	8.61
5	2.02	2.57	4.03	6.87
6	1.94	2.45	3.71	5.96
7	1.90	2.37	3.50	5.41
8	1.86	2.31	3.36	5.04
9	1.83	2.26	3.25	4.78
10	1.81	2.23	3.17	4.59
11	1.80	2.20	3.11	4.44
12	1.78	2.18	3.06	4.32
13	1.77	2.16	3.01	4.22
14	1.76	2.15	2.98	4.14
15	1.75	2.13	2.95	4.07
16	1.75	2.12	2.92	4.02
17	1.74	2.11	2.90	3.97
18	1.73	2.10	2.88	3.92
19	1.73	2.09	2.86	3.88
20	1.73	2.09	2.85	3.85
22	1.72	2.07	2.82	3.79
24	1.71	2.06	2.80	3.75
26	1.71	2.06	2.78	3.71
28	1.70	2.05	2.76	3.67
30	1.70	2.04	2.75	3.65
>30	1.64	1.96	2.58	3.29
Probability that chance could have produced this value of t	0.10	0.05	0.01	0.001
Confidence level	10%	5%	1%	0.1%

Table 10.14: t-test table.

Complete the following:

'The calculated t-value of .... is {*greater than* / *less than*} the critical value of .... for .... degrees of freedom. This means there is a probability of {*<0.05* / *>0.05*} that the difference in reaction time is due to chance. This means there is {*no significant* / *a significant*} difference and the null hypothesis {*is not rejected* / *is rejected*}.'

e   Carry out *t*-tests to determine if there is a significant difference in reaction time when comparing the reflexes. In each case, comment on the level of significance and the validity of the conclusion:

i   touch compared with sound

....

....

....

....

....

ii   sight compared with sound

....

....

....

....

....

Chapter 11

Inheritance, selection and evolution

CHAPTER OUTLINE

This chapter relates to Chapter 16: Inheritance and Chapter 17: Selection and evolution, in the Coursebook.
In this chapter, you will complete practical investigations on:

*   11.1 Studying stages of meiosis in an anther

*   11.2 Modelling the effects of selection pressure on allele frequency

*   11.3 Measuring and comparing continuous variation in two sets of leaves

*   11.4 Investigating tongue-rolling

*   11.5 Modelling the Hardy–Weinberg equations

*   11.6 The effects of selective breeding in *Brassica oleracea*

*   11.7 Comparing vitamin C content in two cultivars of *Brassica oleracea*.

Practical Investigation 11.1: Studying stages of meiosis in an anther

In flowering plants, meiosis takes place in the anthers and ovules. In this investigation, you will study prepared slides of an immature anther, in which diploid pollen mother cells are dividing by meiosis to form haploid cells. You will try to identify cells undergoing different stages of meiosis and make labelled drawings of them.

YOU WILL NEED

Equipment:

• a microscope and light source • prepared slides of immature *Lilium* anther stained to show chromosomes • reference micrographs (e.g. from the internet or textbooks) of cells in various stages of meiosis

Safety considerations

- Make sure you have read the Safety advice section at the beginning of this book and listen to any advice from your teacher before carrying out this investigation.

- There are no significant safety issues associated with this practical investigation.

Method

1   Set up your microscope, and place the slide on the stage. Use a low- or medium-power objective lens to find an area where dividing cells are present. These will be in the centre of the pollen sacs (Figure 11.1).

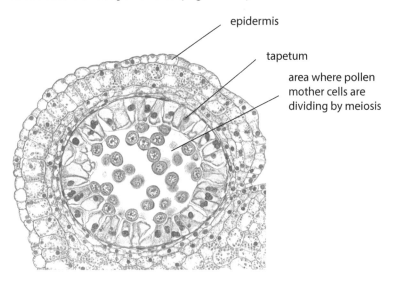

epidermis

tapetum

area where pollen mother cells are dividing by meiosis

Figure 11.1: Photomicrograph of a transverse section of a pollen sac.

2   Swing the high-power objective lens over the slide. Explore the contents of one of the pollen sacs, focusing on the cells undergoing meiosis. Refer to micrographs (in textbooks, or search online) to help you to identify the various stages. The cells are small, so it is not easy to make out the chromosomes (Figure 11.2).

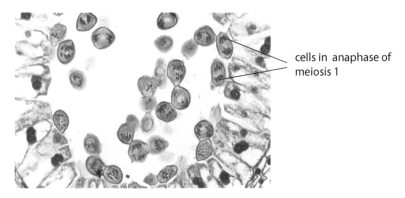

cells in anaphase of meiosis 1

Figure 11.2: Photomicrograph showing dividing cells.

> **TIP**
>
> You may find that all of the cells on your slide are in the same stage of meiosis. If so, try swapping your slide with someone else to find different stages.

3 Make labelled drawings of some of the cells that you can see in the Results section. An example is provided in Figure 11.3.

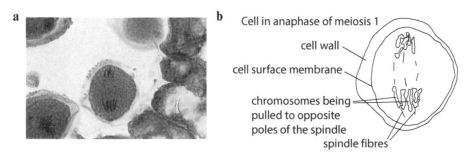

Figure 11.3: Photomicrograph and drawing showing cells in anaphase of meiosis 1.

Results

Practical Investigation 11.2: Modelling the effects of selection pressure on allele frequency

Many genes have different versions, in which the DNA base sequence differs slightly. These are called alleles. Each individual in a population has two copies of the gene, and these two copies may be the same allele (homozygous) or different (heterozygous). Population genetics looks at how common each allele is in the population as a whole. This is known as allele frequency.

In this investigation, you will use different coloured beans (or other small objects) to represent alleles in a population of organisms. You will model what happens when these alleles are passed on to the next generation, as individuals in the population breed randomly with one other. You will then model the effects of different selection pressures against organisms that are homozygous for one of the alleles.

YOU WILL NEED

Equipment:
- at least three different containers • 100 beans of one colour and 100 very similar beans of a second colour

Safety considerations

- Make sure you have read the Safety advice section at the beginning of this book and listen to any advice from your teacher before carrying out this investigation.

- There are no significant safety issues associated with this practical investigation.

Part 1: Investigating allele frequency with no selection pressure

Method

1   The two different colours of beans represent two alleles of a gene, **A** and **a**. **A** is dominant and **a** is recessive. Decide which colour will represent which allele.

    .... beans represent allele ....

    .... beans represent allele ....

2   Begin by assuming that these two alleles are equally common in the population of organisms. Count 100 beans representing the **A** allele, and 100 representing the **a** allele, and place them into the large container. Mix them thoroughly.

3   Without looking, randomly select two beans from the container. These represent two gametes, containing the **A** or **a** alleles, fusing. Put a tally mark for the 'genotype' of the 'zygote' you have produced into the appropriate column of the results table. Put the two beans into a different container.

4   Repeat until you have used up all of the beans in the large container.

Results

Genotype	AA	Aa	aa
Tally			
Number			

Table 11.1: Tally table.

Analysis, conclusion and evaluation

a   What is the ratio between the genotypes of the organisms in the offspring in this population?

    ....

b   What is the ratio between the phenotypes of these offspring?

    ....

c   What is the frequency of the **A** and **a** alleles in these offspring?

    ....

d   If all of these offspring survive and breed together randomly, what would you expect the ratio of genotypes to be in the next generation?

    ....

e   If all of the offspring survive and breed together randomly, what would you expect the frequency of the **A** and **a** alleles to be in the next generation?

    ....

Part 2: Investigating allele frequency in subsequent generations while applying a selection pressure

Method

You are now going to repeat the breeding experiment, but this time you will apply a selection pressure against the homozygous recessive offspring. Your teacher will allocate a particular selection pressure to you.

1   Place all of the 'offspring' from Part 1 back into the container and mix them thoroughly.

2   Randomly pull out pairs of 'alleles' as before. Remove pairs of **aa** alleles
    according to the selection pressure you are applying. Some examples are shown in
    Table 11.2.

Selection pressure	Action
50%	remove every second pair of **aa** alleles
25%	remove every fourth pair of **aa** alleles
20%	remove every fifth pair of **aa** alleles
10%	remove every tenth pair of **aa** alleles

Table 11.2: Breeding experiment: effect of selection pressure.

Put the alleles you have removed into a different container – they have died before
they can reproduce, and so will not contribute to the next generation.

On a piece of rough paper, tally the numbers of the **AA**, **Aa** and **aa** genotypes
produced. Record the numbers of offspring of each genotype, and the numbers of
a alleles discarded, in Table 11.3.

3   Put the surviving offspring back into the container and mix them up again. Repeat
    Step 2 to obtain results for Generation 2.

4   Repeat Steps 2 and 3 until you have results for six generations.

Results

selection pressure applied ....

Generation	Number of AA genotype	Number of Aa genotype	Number of aa genotype	Number of a alleles removed
1				
2				
3				
4				
5				
6				

Table 11.3: Results table.

Analysis, conclusion and evaluation

a   Use your results in Table 11.3 to complete Table 11.4.

Generation	Number of a alleles remaining in the population	Total number of both alleles remaining in the population	Percentage of allele a in the population	Frequency of allele a in the population
0	100	200	50	0.50
1				
2				
3				
4				
5				
6				

Table 11.4: Calculated results table.

b Plot a graph of your results with generation number on the *x*-axis, and frequency of allele **a** on the *y*-axis.

c Collect data from other groups who have exerted different selection pressures. Plot and draw lines for their results on your graph in **b**.

d Describe the results you obtained. You should refer to Tables 11.3 and 11.4, as well as your graph, in your answer.

....

....

....

....

....

....

e If you applied a 100% selection pressure against the homozygous recessive (**aa**) offspring, would allele **a** immediately disappear from the population? Explain your answer.

....

....

....

f Discuss the extent to which this model can be considered to truly represent changes in allele frequency in a breeding population of living organisms.

....

....

....

....

....

....

....

....

Practical Investigation 11.3: Measuring and comparing continuous variation in two sets of leaves

Differences between the phenotypes of individuals of the same species are known as variation. In continuous variation, each individual can have any value between the extremes of the range – there are no distinct categories. Continuous variation can be affected by genes if many different genes have an effect on that feature, or if there are many different alleles of genes. Continuous variation is also often the result of differing environmental factors affecting a feature.

In this investigation, you will measure variation in leaf length. You will collect samples of leaves that have experienced a difference in their environment, and will use statistical tests to determine whether any differences between these two sets of leaves are significant.

YOU WILL NEED

Equipment:
- access to leaves of the same species that experience a difference in their environment – for example, on the sunny and shady sides of a tree • ruler to measure in mm • small bags to put the leaves into as you collect them

Safety considerations

- Make sure you have read the Safety advice section at the beginning of this book and listen to any advice from your teacher before carrying out this investigation.

- Work in pairs to collect leaves from the tree.

- Select a tree where you can reach the leaves without having to climb onto anything.

Method

1   Write down the environmental factor that differs for the two samples of leaves that you will collect.

   ....

2   Collect 30 leaves from each of the two different environments.

   Explain how you will ensure that the only variable between your two samples is the environmental factor you are investigating.

   ....

   ....

TIP

Make sure that you keep the two sets of leaves separate from one another, and that you know which set is which!

....

....

3 Measure the length of each leaf, and record your results as two lists, or in two results tables, in the Results section.

4 Look at the range of measurements that you have made. Decide on suitable categories into which you can organise these measurements.

You should have at least five categories for each sample, and the range of lengths within each category should be the same.

Use your measurements to record the number of leaves within each category.

Record your results in the Results section, one for each set of leaves.

<table>
<tr><td>TIP</td></tr>
<tr><td>If you do not have time to collect 30 leaves from each place, or if there are not enough leaves to collect, just collect as many as you can. Try to collect the same number of leaves in each set.</td></tr>
</table>

Results

Analysis, conclusion and evaluation

a Draw frequency diagrams (histograms) to display your results. Use the grid on the next page.

TIP

Remember that bars touch in a frequency diagram (histogram).

b Calculate the mean length of the leaves from *each* set.

Mean length for the set of leaves from .... = ...

Mean length for the set of leaves from .... = ...

c Plot a bar chart to show the mean lengths of each set of leaves.

> **TIP**
>
> Remember to use the same number of significant figures, or one more than, in your answer as in the individual measurements.

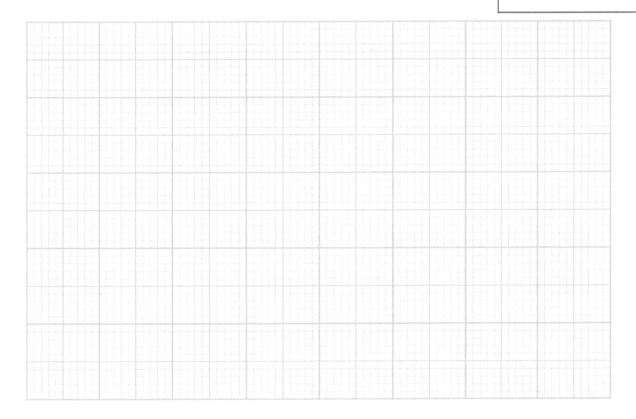

d Calculate the standard deviation for *each* of your sets of data, using the formula:

$$s = \sqrt{\frac{\Sigma(x - \bar{x})^2}{n - 1}}$$

> **TIP**
>
> Remember that bars do not touch in a bar chart.

where:

s = standard deviation

x = each individual measurement

$\bar{x}$ = the mean

n = the number of measurements made

Standard deviation for set of leaves from .... = ...

Standard deviation for set of leaves from .... = ...

e   Calculate standard error, SE, for each set of leaves, using the formula:

$$SE = \frac{s}{\sqrt{n}}$$

Show your working.

TIP

You can use a calculator, app or website to calculate standard deviation.

Standard error for set of leaves from .... = ...

Standard error for set of leaves from .... = ...

f   Return to the bar chart that you drew in **c**. On each bar, draw an error bar that extends above and below the top of the bar, to a distance of 2 × the standard error (see Figure 11.4).

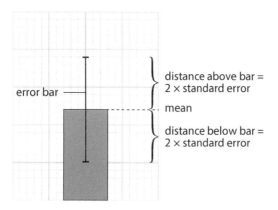

error bar

distance above bar = 2 × standard error

mean

distance below bar = 2 × standard error

Figure 11.4: Method for plotting error bars.

g   If the error bars on your bar chart for the two samples overlap, this indicates that any difference in the means of the two samples could be due to chance.

What do your error bars suggest about your two samples?

....

....

....

h   You can also do a *t*-test to determine whether any difference between the mean values of your two samples is significant.

The formula for the *t*-test is:

$$t = \frac{|\bar{x}_1 - \bar{x}_2|}{\sqrt{\left(\dfrac{s_1^2}{n_1} + \dfrac{s_2^2}{n_2}\right)}}$$

You have already calculated:

- the means for the two samples, $\bar{x}_1$ and $\bar{x}_2$
- the standard deviations for the two samples, s_1 and s_2
- you know that n_1 and n_2 are the number of leaves in each of the two samples.

Calculate t.

Show your working.

i   The null hypothesis for this investigation is:

   there is no difference between the mean lengths of the two sets of leaves.

Determine the degrees of freedom, v, in your data, using the formula:

$$v = n_1 + n_2 - 2$$

Degrees of freedom = ...

j   Use Table 11.5 to find the probability that the null hypothesis is correct, for your calculated value of t. The numbers in the table are values of t.

Degrees of freedom	Probability that the null hypothesis is correct (i.e. probability that chance produced the difference between the two means)			
	0.10	0.05	0.01	0.001
1	6.31	12.7	63.7	63.6
5	2.02	2.57	4.03	6.87
10	1.81	2.23	3.17	4.59
15	1.75	2.13	2.95	4.07
20	1.73	2.09	2.85	3.85
25	1.71	2.06	2.78	3.71
30	1.70	2.04	2.75	3.65
more than 30	1.64	1.96	2.58	3.29

Table 11.5: Probability table.

Probability that null hypothesis is correct for the circled value of t = ...

k   Summarise what the t-test tells you about the difference between the means of the lengths of the leaves from the two different environments.

....

....

....

....

....

Practical Investigation 11.4: Investigating tongue-rolling

Some people are able to roll their tongue (Figure 11.5).

Many textbooks state that tongue rolling shows discontinuous variation, and is determined only by genes and not by environment.

You are going to plan and carry out an investigation to test the hypothesis:

> the ability to roll the tongue is not affected by environment.

In your plan, consider:

- what you will measure or count, and how you will do this

- how you will try to determine whether environment (e.g. learning, practising) can affect the ability to roll the tongue

- what is your independent variable, your dependent variable, and the key variables to try to standardise

- any significant risks in your procedure and how you will deal with them

- the size of the sample that you will use

- how you will record, display and analyse your results.

You should also evaluate the reliability of any conclusions that you make from your data. Finally, you may be able to suggest how you could improve your investigation if you had sufficient time to do it again.

Figure 11.5 Woman rolling her tongue.

Method

....

....

....

....

....

....

....

....

....

....

....

....

....

....

....

....

....

....

Results

Analysis, conclusion and evaluation

....

....

....

....

....

....

....

....

....

....

....

....

....

....

....

....

....

....

....

....

....

....

....

....

....

....

....

....

....

....

....

....

....

....

....

....

....

....

....

....

....

....

....

....

....

....

....

Practical Investigation 11.5: Modelling the Hardy–Weinberg equations

The Hardy–Weinberg equations are two simple equations that involve the frequency of two alleles of a gene. The equations allow you to calculate the frequencies of the alleles in a population, and also the frequencies of the homozygous and heterozygous genotypes.

In this exercise you will use the same modelling technique as in Practical Investigation 11.2.

Part 1: Modelling the equations with all conditions satisfied

You will, first of all, determine if the Hardy–Weinberg equations are correct in predicting the frequencies of different genotypes in a population. You will then investigate some circumstances that can mean that the Hardy–Weinberg equations do not apply to populations.

The two equations are:

$$p + q = 1$$

where p is the frequency of the dominant allele of the gene, and q is the frequency of the recessive allele and

$$p^2 + 2pq + q^2 = 1$$

where p^2 is the frequency of the dominant homozygous genotype, $2pq$ is the frequency of the heterozygous genotype and q^2 is the frequency of the other homozygous genotype.

YOU WILL NEED

Equipment:

- 150 beans of one type, and 50 of another; the two types of beans should be as similar in size, shape and texture as possible, but should differ in colour
- several containers, for example beakers

Safety considerations

- Make sure you have read the Safety advice section at the beginning of this book and listen to any advice from your teacher before carrying out this investigation.
- There are no significant safety issues associated with this practical investigation.

Method

1 Count 150 beans of one colour, and 50 beans of another colour, into a container.

2 Follow the method described in Practical Investigation 11.2, Part 1 Method. Continue for at least three generations.

Results

Tally the numbers of each genotype in each generation. Add up your tallies and record the numbers of each genotype in each generation in a results table here.

Analysis, conclusion and evaluation

a For each generation, you should have 100 'offspring' in total.

For each generation, calculate the percentage of **AA**, **Aa** and **aa** offspring.

Convert the percentages to frequencies.

Record your results in Table 11.6.

> **TIP**
>
> How many alleles (beans) do you have altogether? How many of these are allele **A** beans? So what percentage of the total do the allele **A** beans make up? Convert this percentage to a frequency.

Generation	Total number of offspring	Percentage of AA offspring	Frequency of AA offspring	Percentage of Aa offspring	Frequency of Aa offspring	Percentage of aa offspring	Frequency of aa offspring
1	100						
2	100						
3	100						

Table 11.6: Results table.

Determine whether your results, for each generation, fit the Hardy–Weinberg equations, as follows.

b p is the frequency of allele **A**. What is p in your model?

....

c q is the frequency of allele **a**. What is q in your model?

....

d In the Hardy–Weinberg equations, p^2 is the frequency of **AA** genotypes.

Calculate p^2 by squaring your value of p.

....

e Does this calculated value match the frequency of the **AA** genotype in each generation in your results?

....

....

f In the Hardy–Weinberg equations, q^2 is the frequency of **aa** genotypes.

Calculate q^2 by squaring your value of q.

....

g   Does this calculated value match the frequency of the **aa** genotype in each generation in your results?

....

....

h   In the Hardy–Weinberg equations, $2pq$ is the frequency of the **Aa** genotype. Calculate $2pq$. ....

i   Does this calculated value match the frequency of the **Aa** genotype in each generation in your results?

....

....

Part 2: Modelling the equations with one or more conditions *not* satisfied

The Hardy–Weinberg equations only apply when certain conditions are true for a population. These conditions include:

* mating between individuals in the population is random

* no new mutations occur

* there is no immigration or emigration

* all individuals have an equal chance of surviving and reproducing – that is, no selection occurs.

You are now going to use the same technique to model what happens to allele frequencies over time if one of these conditions is *not* fulfilled.

You have already modelled the effect of natural selection on allele frequency, in Practical Investigation 11.2.

Your teacher will give you a particular condition.

Plan how you can adapt the technique used in the first part of this investigation, to find out whether or not the Hardy–Weinberg equations still apply, when this condition is *not* met.

Condition you will investigate:

....

Hypothesis you will test:

....

....

Method

....

....

....

....

....

....

....

....

....

....

....

....

....

Results

Analysis, conclusion and evaluation

....

....

....

....

....

....

....

....

....

....

....

....

....

....

....

....

Practical Investigation 11.6: The effects of selective breeding in *Brassica oleracea*

Brassica oleracea is a plant that grows wild in southern and western Europe. Its common English name is wild cabbage (Figure 11.6).

Figure 11.6: *Brassica oleracea.*

B. oleracea is an important food crop in many parts of the world. It is thought to have been grown for thousands of years, and during this time many different varieties (cultivars) have been produced by selective breeding. These include cabbage, kale, Brussels sprouts, kohlrabi, cauliflower, broccoli and kai-lan.

In this investigation, you will compare the structure (morphology) of some varieties of *B. oleracea* that have been produced by selective breeding.

YOU WILL NEED

Equipment:
- three or more different cultivars of *B. oleracea* • ruler to measure in mm

---

Safety considerations
- Make sure you have read the Safety advice section at the beginning of this book and listen to any advice from your teacher before carrying out this investigation.
- There are no significant safety issues associated with this practical investigation.

Method

1   Prepare the space in the results section to compare three cultivars of *B. oleracea*. You should select at least *five* different features to compare. Try to make at least one of your comparisons quantitative.

Results

Analysis, conclusion and evaluation

a   Select *one* of the cultivars of *B. oleracea* that you have been given.
Outline how selective breeding could have produced this cultivar from wild
cabbage.

....

....

....

....

....

....

....

....

....

....

> TIP
>
> In some cultivars, particular plant parts have become enlarged or changed in shape and form. It will be helpful to identify these parts in your chosen cultivar. If you cannot work this out just from looking at the specimen, use the internet to find more information.

Practical Investigation 11.7: Comparing vitamin C content in two cultivars of *Brassica oleracea*

All cultivars of *B. oleracea* are rich in vitamin C (ascorbic acid).

Vitamin C is an oxidising agent. It oxidises a solution of purple DCPIP to a colourless compound. The greater the quantity of vitamin C, the greater the quantity of DCPIP that can be decolourised.

Plan and carry out an investigation to compare the vitamin C content of two cultivars of *B. oleracea*.

Planning

Write down a null hypothesis for your investigation.

....

....

Variables

independent variable:

....

dependent variable:

....

variables to be standardised:

....

....

....

> **YOU WILL NEED**
>
> **List the equipment you will need. Draw a labelled diagram of how you will set up the equipment.**
>
> ....
>
> ....
>
> ....

Safety considerations

List any risks associated with your planned procedure.

For each risk, outline how you will minimise it.

....

....

....

....

....

Method

Describe how you will carry out your investigation.

....

....

....

> **TIP**
>
> Think about the statistical test that you might want to do to determine whether any differences that you find are significant. For example, if you plan to use a *t*-test, you will need at least ten samples from each *Brassica* cultivar.

....

....

....

....

....

....

Results

Record your results in a suitable table.

Analysis, conclusion and evaluation

a   Analyse your results in a suitable way. For example, you may decide to draw a graph.

If you have analysed several samples from each cultivar, you may be able to carry out a statistical analysis to determine whether any differences that you have found between the two cultivars are significant.

....

....

....

....

....

....

....

....

....

....

....

....

....

b Discuss the reliability of your results and conclusion.

....

....

....

....

....

....

....

....

....

....

....

....

....

Chapter 12

Ecology

This chapter relates to Chapter 18: Classificiation, biodiversity and conservation, in the Coursebook.

In this chapter, you will complete practical investigations on:

- 12.1 Using frame quadrats to assess abundance of organisms

- 12.2 Using frame quadrats to compare biodiversity in two habitats

- 12.3 Using a transect to investigate distribution and abundance of species

- 12.4 Investigating a possible correlation between species distribution and an abiotic factor

- 12.5 Estimating the population size of a small, mobile invertebrate.

Practical Investigation 12.1: Using frame quadrats to assess abundance of organisms

A **population** is a group of organisms of the same species, living in the same place at the same time. We can estimate the **abundance** of different species of plants, or of sedentary animals (ones that remain in one place) using quadrats.

It is usually not possible to count every single organism in a population. Instead, you can **sample** the population. This means that you count the organisms in a small but representative part of the whole area. A **quadrat** is simply a square frame within which you sample the organisms.

In this practical investigation, you will use **random sampling**. This type of sampling is used when you want to estimate the population of a species in a reasonably uniform area. You place the quadrats randomly in order to ensure that your sampled areas are representative of the whole area.

YOU WILL NEED

Equipment:
- quadrat with sides of 0.50m • two long measuring tapes • a list of random numbers, or a method for generating them (e.g. a phone app)

KEY WORDS

population: a group of organisms of the same species, living in the same place at the same time

abundance: how many individuals of a species are present in an area

sample: a small part of the whole, from which data is collected when it is not possible to count or measure the whole

quadrat: a frame that marks out an area within which data is collected

random sampling: taking samples from randomly chosen areas within the whole area

Safety considerations

- Make sure you have read the Safety advice section at the beginning of this book and listen to any advice from your teacher before carrying out this investigation.

- When working outside, always work with a partner.

- Check with your teacher to find out whether you are likely to find any poisonous plants, or ones that you may be allergic to. If in any doubt, wear gloves.

Method

1 Select an area of ground that you will investigate. This could be a grassy area (e.g. a playing field, a lawn or a meadow), a rocky shore, a sand dune, or any other suitable habitat that is available to you. Walk around the area, to get a general idea of what plants are growing there, or what sedentary animals are present.

2 Use the long measuring tapes to mark out a large area within which you will sample the organisms. Arrange the tapes at right angles to one another, so that one of them represents an *x*-axis and one represents a *y*-axis (Figure 12.1).

3 Use a random number generator to provide you with two numbers, for example 14 and 6. Use these as coordinates, with the first number representing the *x*-axis value and the second number the *y*-axis value. Place your quadrat with its bottom left-hand corner at the point within the 'axes' specified by the coordinates.

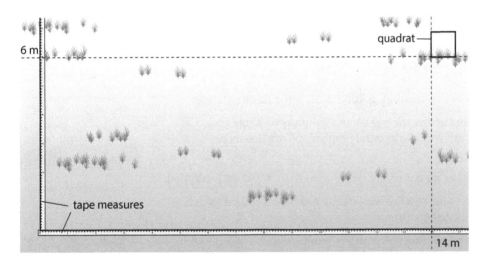

Figure 12.1: Method for investigation 12.1.

4 Now you need to measure and record what is inside your quadrat. How you do this will depend on the kinds of organisms that you are recording.

- If you are working with organisms that you can clearly see as individuals, you can simply record the number of them in the quadrat. This works well on a rocky shore, for example, where you can count sedentary animals such as limpets or periwinkles.

- If you are working in a grassy area, it is usually not possible to count the numbers of individual plants, because you cannot tell where one plant stops and another one starts. Instead, you can estimate the percentage of the area of the quadrat that is covered by each species. This is called **percentage cover**. To help you to do this, you can use a quadrat that is divided up into smaller squares (Figure 12.2) – it is much easier to estimate the coverage within several small squares than in one big one.

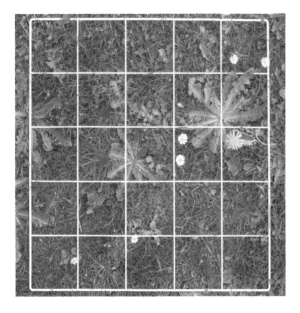

Figure 12.2: Method for assessing percentage cover.

- Record your data for the first quadrat in Table 12.1 in the results section.

Insert an appropriate heading across the right-hand columns of Table 12.1, depending on whether you are recording actual numbers of organisms or percentage cover.

Beneath this heading, write the names of the species you have found and recorded.

5   Repeat Steps 3 and 4 at least nine more times, so that you have a record from a minimum of 10 randomly placed quadrats.

Add more columns, on a separate sheet of paper, if you have more than 13 species in your samples, and more rows if you have recorded samples from more than 10 quadrats.

<aside>

KEY WORD

percentage cover: the percentage of the sampled area that is covered by the species being recorded

TIP

Another way of estimating organisms that you cannot count as individuals is to use an abundance scale, such as the Braun–Blanquet scale:

+ = less than 1% cover
1 = 1–4% cover
2 = 5–25% cover
3 = 26–50% cover
4 = 51–75% cover
5 = 76–100% cover

TIP

It is great if you can name all of the species within your quadrat, but this is not essential. If you do not know their names, you can simply refer to them as Species A, Species B and so on.

</aside>

Results

Quadrat													
1													
2													
3													
4													
5													
6													
7													
8													
9													
10													

Table 12.1: Results table.

Analysis, conclusion and evaluation

a   Calculate the mean number, or mean percentage cover, for each of the species in your samples.

Add these as a final row in Table 12.1.

b   If you have counted numbers of organisms, you can estimate the population size of each species in the habitat.

   i   Measure, or estimate if precise measurement is not possible, the total area of the habitat.

Total area of habitat = ...

   ii   Calculate the total area you sampled with your quadrats. (For example, if each quadrat had sides of 0.50 m, and you used 10 quadrats, the total area sampled is $0.50 \times 0.50 \times 10 = 2.5\,\text{m}^2$.)

Total area sampled = ...

   iii   Calculate the estimated number of individuals of each species in the whole habitat:

$$\text{total number of individuals in Species A} = \frac{\text{total area of habitat}}{\text{area sampled}} \times \text{number of individuals of Species A in sample}$$

Estimated number of individuals of Species A in the whole habitat = ………….

c   Identify the major sources of error in your investigation.

   ....

   ....

   ....

   ....

   ....

   ....

d   Suggest how the investigation could be improved, to provide a true value of the abundance of each of the species in your samples.

   ....

   ....

   ....

   ....

   ....

   ....

   ....

   ....

Practical Investigation 12.2: Using frame quadrats to compare biodiversity in two habitats

Biodiversity is a difficult term to define. It includes the range of different ecosystems in an area, the range of different habitats in an ecosystem, the range of different species in a habitat and the range of genetic diversity within these species.

In this investigation, you will measure the number of different species, and the numbers of individual organisms in each species, in two different habitats. You will then use Simpson's Index of Diversity to calculate a diversity index for each habitat.

YOU WILL NEED

Equipment:
- quadrat with sides of 0.50m • two long measuring tapes

Safety considerations

- Make sure you have read the Safety advice section at the beginning of this book and listen to any advice from your teacher before carrying out this investigation.

- When working outside, always work with a partner.

- Check with your teacher to find out whether you are likely to find any poisonous plants, or ones that you may be allergic to. If in any doubt, wear gloves.

Method

1   Select the two areas where you are going to work. Choose areas where you can count individual organisms, rather than using percentage cover. For example, you could investigate:

- two areas on a rocky shore, at different heights above the sea, or facing different aspects (e.g. north and west)

- two areas of waste ground where countable plants are growing, with different factors affecting them (e.g. one where people regularly walk and one where they do not, or one that is in the sun and one that is in the shade).

areas to be sampled:

....

....

2   Use randomly placed quadrats, as in Practical Investigation 12.1, to sample both areas. Use the same number of quadrats, of the same size, in each area.

Results

Record your results for both areas in the following space.

Analysis, conclusion and evaluation

a   Add up the total number of individuals of each species that you have counted in all the quadrats in each area.

Use your results to complete Table 12.2.

Add more rows if you have counted more than 10 species.

Species	Number in Area 1	Number in Area 2

Table 12.2: Results table.

b   The formula for Simpson's index of diversity, D, is:

$$D = 1 - \left(\Sigma \left(\frac{n}{N} \right)^2 \right)$$

where:

n is the number of organisms of each species in one area

N is the total number of individuals of all species in one area

First, concentrate on Area 1.

Calculate the total number of individuals of all species in Area 1.

Total number of individuals of all species, N, in Area 1 = ...

c   Copy your results from Table 12.2 into Table 12.3. Calculate n/N and $(n/N)^2$ for each species and complete the table. Record each number to three decimal places.

> **TIP**
>
> You could set up and use a spreadsheet, for example on Excel, to do these calculations.

Species	Number, n	$n \div N$	$(n \div N)^2$

Table 12.3: Area 1: calculated results table.

d Add up all the values of $(n \div N)^2$, to find $\Sigma(n \div N)^2$.

$\Sigma(n \div N)^2 =$ ....

e Find the diversity index by subtracting your answer to **d** from 1:

$1 - \Sigma(n \div N)^2 =$ ....

f Repeat Steps **b–e**, using Table 12.4 to find Simpson's diversity index for Area 2.

Species	Number, n	$n \div N$	$(n \div N)^2$

Table 12.4: Area 2: calculated results table.

> ### TIP
>
> The diversity index you have calculated should lie between 0 and 1. If it does not, you have gone wrong somewhere! The closer the number is to 1, the greater the species diversity in the area.

g Summarise what your results indicate about the biodiversity of the two areas you have studied.

....

....

....

....

h Suggest how your investigation could be improved, to increase confidence in your results.

....

....

....

....

Practical Investigation 12.3: Using a transect to investigate distribution and abundance of species

In Practical Investigations 12.1 and 12.2, you used random sampling to measure the abundance of different species in a particular area. Sometimes, however, we want to know if the abundance of organisms is different in different parts of a habitat. This is often done when there is gradual change in the conditions in the habitat – for example, from a wet area to a drier area, or from sunshine into shade, or from the top of the shore to sea level. We want to know about the **distribution** of the organisms, as well as their abundance.

In this investigation, you will use quadrats to sample organisms along a line, called a transect. This is **systematic sampling**. You will measure their abundance at intervals along the transect, which will give you information about their distribution.

> **KEY WORDS**
>
> **distribution:** where a species is found in a habitat
>
> **systematic sampling:** taking samples at predetermined points

YOU WILL NEED

Equipment:
- quadrat with sides of 0.50m • a long measuring tape • string • pegs to hold string in place

Safety considerations

- Make sure you have read the Safety advice section at the beginning of this book and listen to any advice from your teacher before carrying out this investigation.

- When working outside, always work with a partner.

- Check with your teacher to find out whether you are likely to find any poisonous plants, or ones that you may be allergic to. If in any doubt, wear gloves.

Method

1   Select a line along which you will sample your organisms. Place a long piece of string along your chosen line. Peg the string down firmly at intervals.

2   Decide whether you will use a **line transect**, a **continuous belt transect** or an **interrupted belt transect** (Figure 12.3). This will depend on the length of your transect, the types of organisms you are sampling, and the time you have available.

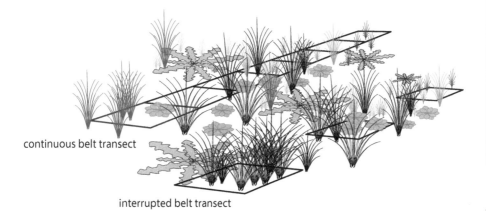

continuous belt transect

interrupted belt transect

Figure 12.3: Method for investigation 12.3.

- For a line transect, you do not use quadrats. You simply record every species that is touching the string, along its whole length.

- For a continuous belt transect, place the quadrat against the string. Record the abundance of each species in it, either by counting, using percentage cover, or an abundance scale. Then move the quadrat along the string, without leaving a space between the first and second placing. Continue all along the string.

- For an interrupted belt transect, leave regular spaces between the quadrat placements.

3   Decide how you can record your results clearly and systematically. Construct a suitable results table in the space below.

TIP

The length of your transect will depend on the area you are studying. Also consider how much time you have – do not make the transect so long that you will not have time to sample all the way along it.

Results

Analysis, conclusion and evaluation

a Draw a **kite diagram** to display your results.

Figure 12.4 shows an example of a kite diagram for a rocky shore, where the abundance of the organisms was estimated using the Braun–Blanquet scale.

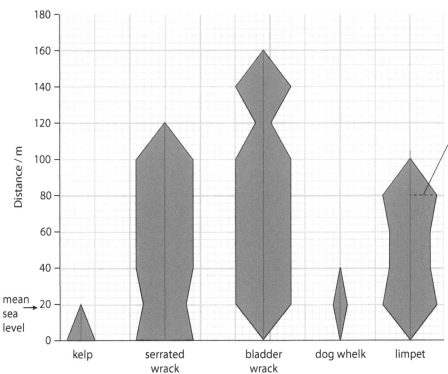

This shows that limpets had a Braun–Blanquet value of 4 at a distance of 80 m up the shore.

Figure 12.4: Kite diagram for a rocky shore.

When drawing a kite diagram:

- Use graph paper.

- Decide which way round you want your 'kites' to run. You can have distance on the *y*-axis and species on the *x*-axis, as in Figure 12.4. Alternatively, you can have distance on the *x*-axis and species on the *y*-axis, so that the kites run across the page rather than up and down.

- Construct the distance scale, according to the length of the transect you have used.

- List the species along the other scale, spacing them evenly apart. Think about how much space you need for each species – read the next bullet point before doing this.

- Each 'kite' shows the abundance of that species at different distances along the line. Use a ruler to draw a faint pencil line vertically upwards, or horizontally, from the centre position of each species. Then use your results to plot points representing the numbers, percentage cover or abundance of that species at each measured position, *on both sides* of this central line.

- Join your points with ruled straight lines, to make symmetrical shapes centred on the pencil line you have drawn for each species.

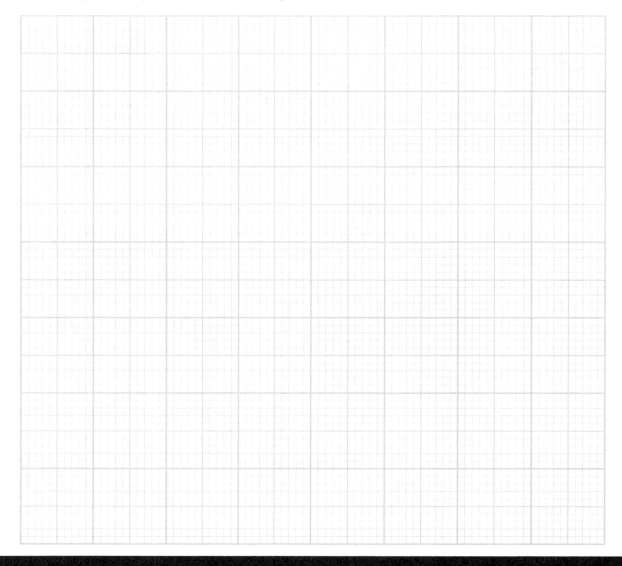

b Select **two** species that show different distributions along your transect.
Describe the distribution of each of these species.

....

....

....

....

....

c Suggest reasons for the distributions that you have described in **b.** You could
consider how environmental factors vary along the transect, and how the
adaptations of the species may help them to survive in particular environments.

....

....

....

....

....

....

....

....

....

....

....

....

....

....

....

d Explain why you chose the type of transect that you decided to use for this investigation.

....

....

....

....

....

Practical Investigation 12.4: Investigating a possible correlation between species distribution and an abiotic factor

Some species have very particular requirements – they can only live in habitats where their adaptations are suited for survival within a particular range of environmental factors. In this investigation, you will plan an investigation to measure the abundance of a species and a chosen environmental factor, and look for any correlation between them.

For example:

- plant Species A may be more abundant where light levels are high than where light levels are low

- plant Species B may be more abundant where soil moisture levels are low than where they are high.

You may be able to use your results from Practical Investigation 12.3 to give you a starting point. Perhaps you found that a particular species seems to be more abundant in one part of the transect than another. Is there a possible abiotic factor that could explain this? Your hypothesis could be constructed from these earlier results.

Planning

When planning your investigation, you will need to think about:

- which species and factor you will investigate

- how you will measure the abiotic factor (e.g. using a light meter)

- how you will measure the abundance of the organism in different areas – would random or systematic sampling be best?

- how you will analyse your results to determine whether there is a correlation between the abiotic factor and the abundance of the species.

> TIP

Spearman's rank correlation is described in Practical Investigation 8.2 in this Workbook. For information about how to use Pearson's linear correlation, see Chapter P2 in the Cambridge AS & A Level Biology Coursebook or Exercise 18.2 in the Cambridge AS & A Level Biology Workbook.

The results analysis should use either Spearman's rank correlation or Pearson's linear correlation. You will need to plan your investigation so that the data you collect are suitable for use with one of these tests. This means that you will need at least ten pairs of readings, with each pair including a measurement for the abundance of the organism and a measurement for the abiotic factor.

YOU WILL NEED

List the equipment you will need:

- .... • ....

- .... • ....

- .... • ....

Safety considerations

What precautions will you take to make sure that the investigation is performed safely?

....

....

....

Method

....

....

....

....

....

....

....

....

....

....

....

....

....

....

....

....

....

....

Results

Analysis, conclusion and evaluation

a   Plot a scattergram of the values of the measured abiotic factor against the numbers of the organism. If you think you can see a correlation, decide whether it is linear or non-linear.

b Use either Spearman's rank correlation or Pearson's linear correlation to analyse your results. The formulae are shown below. Show your working clearly.

Spearman's rank correlation:

$$r_s = 1 - \left(\frac{6 \times \Sigma D^2}{n^3 - n} \right)$$

where:

r_s = Spearman's rank correlation

D = the difference between each pair of ranked measurements

n = the number of pairs of items in the sample

Pearson's linear correlation:

$$r = \frac{\Sigma xy - n\bar{x}\,\bar{y}}{(n-1)s_x s_y}$$

where:

r = Pearson's rank correlation n = total number of observations

x and y = individual observations s_x and s_y = standard deviation for x and y

$\bar{x}$ and $\bar{y}$ = means of x and y

c   Explain what the results of the statistical test mean.

....

....

....

....

d   Suggest how your investigation could be improved to increase confidence in the results.

....

....

....

....

....

....

....

Practical Investigation 12.5: Estimating the population size of a small, mobile invertebrate

In this investigation, you will use the Lincoln Index, also known as the Petersen index, to estimate the number of animals in a local population. This technique is also known as the mark–release–recapture technique.

The animals should be mobile – the method only works if they move around and mix up with each other after you have marked them. Possible animals you could investigate include woodlice or snails.

You need to take care to choose a suitable method of marking the animals. It must not harm them in any way, and ideally it should not make them more visible or attractive to predators. A dull colour of non-toxic paint, applied with a small brush, often works well.

> **YOU WILL NEED**
>
> **Equipment:**
> • small containers, preferably with lids • non-toxic paint and a small brush, or other method of marking • if required, gloves or equipment for handling the animals that will not harm them (e.g. blunt forceps).

Safety considerations

- Make sure you have read the Safety advice section at the beginning of this book and listen to any advice from your teacher before carrying out this investigation.

- When working outside, always work with a partner.

- If you live in an area where there are animals that can give a harmful bite or sting, take great care when searching.

Method

1   Make sure that you can identify the type of animal that you are investigating, and you know the types of places it is likely to be found. Decide on the area within which you want to estimate the population size. Explore the area, and decide on the places where you will search, trying to cover as much of the area as possible in the time available to you.

2   Search carefully. Try to capture at least 30 individual animals.

   As soon as you have captured an animal, mark it with your chosen method. Immediately release it back into the place that you found it. Keep a running total of the number of animals that you mark.

   Total number of animals marked in first sample ....

3   Return to the same site after 24 h or more. (The animals need to be given time to redistribute themselves and mix with unmarked animals in the population.) Capture as many animals as you can in the time available to you. Record the number of marked and unmarked animals that you capture in the tally chart below.

Results

	Marked animals in second sample	Unmarked animals in second sample
Tally		
Number		

Table 12.5: Tally table.

Analysis, conclusion and evaluation

a   Calculate the estimated number of animals in the whole population, using the formula:

$$\text{number in population} = \frac{\text{number caught and marked in first sample} \times \text{total number in second sample}}{\text{number of marked animals in second sample}}$$

Show your working.

b   List reasons why your calculation may not provide a true value for the size of the population of this animal.

....

....

....

....

....

....

....

....

> Glossary

abundance: how many individuals of a species are present in an area.

Benedict's solution: a test for the presence of reducing sugars; the unknown substance is heated with Benedict's reagent, and a change from a clear blue solution to the production of a yellow, red or brown precipitate indicates the presence of reducing sugars such as glucose

best-fit line: a smooth line which shows the trend that the points seem to ft. There is not a single perfect place to put a best-fit line, but you should ensure that approximately the same number of points, roughly the same distances from the line, lie above and below it initial rate of reaction

Biuret test: a test for the presence of amine groups and thus for the presence of proteins; biuret reagent is added to the unknown substance, and a change from pale blue to purple indicates the presence of proteins

buffer solution: a solution that has a known pH, which can be added to a reacting mixture to maintain the pH at that level.

calibrate: convert the readings on a scale to a standard scale with known units

chromatography: a method for the separation of a mixture of substances according to the speed with which they move through a medium, such as chromatography paper.

95% confidence limits: a measure of how accurate a mean value is. There is a 95% probability that the true mean lies between ± 2 standard errors of the mean.

continuous belt transect: a line along which sampling is done by placing quadrats at every position along the line.

continuous variables: variables that are quantitative and can have any value within an interval; for example, length or mass are continuous variables.

correlation: a relationship, or connection, between two variables. Correlations may be positive (if one varable increases so does the other) or negative (if one variable increases, the other decreases.)

dependent variable: the variable that the experiment is measuring (and that changes as a result of changing the independent variable).

distribution: where a species is found in a habitat.

error bars: there is a 95% certainty that the true mean lies within the range of an error bar that extends two standard errors above the mean and two standard errors below the mean.

eyepiece graticule: small scale that is placed in a microscope eyepiece

erythrocytes (red blood cells): these are the largest number of cells and appear spherical with a paler centre.

independent variable: the variable (factor) that is deliberately changed in an experiment.

iodine test: a test for starch. Iodine solution turns a blue-black colour in the presence of starch

interrupted belt transect: a line along which sampling is done by placing quadrats at regular intervals along the line.

kite diagram: a chart showing how the abundance of species varies at measured points in a habitat.

line transect: a line along which sampling is done.

lymphocytes (white blood cells): these are smaller, spherical cells with a large circular nucleus that takes up a large proportion of the cell.

macerate: to break something up in water.

magnification: the number of times larger an image of an object is than the real size of the object

meristem: a part of a plant where cells are actively dividing.

monocytes (white blood cells): these are large cells with a nucleus that is large and often kidney-shaped.

neutrophils (white blood cells): these are large cells with a lobed nucleus.

null hypothesis: a hypothesis that assumes there is no relationship between two variables, or that there is no significant difference between two samples.

oxidising agent: a substance that removes electrons from another substance **qualitative test:** a test that gives a non-numerical description of something (e.g. the intensity of a colour)

Pearson's linear correlation: a statistical test used to determine whether two variables show a linear correlation.

percentage cover: the percentage of the sampled area that is covered by the species being recorded.

plan diagrams: a low power diagram of something that shows tissues but not individual cells.

population: a group of organisms or the same species, living in the same place at the same time.

quadrat: a frame that marks out an area within which data is collected.

quantitative test: a test that gives a precise, numerical description of something (e.g. a glucose concentration of 0.015%).

random error: a source of uncertainty in your results that gives incorrect values that can be of different magnitudes; random errors can affect trends shown by results.

random sampling: taking samples from randomly chosen areas within the whole area.

range: the spread between the lowest and highest value.

R_f value: a number that indicates how far a substance travels during chromatography, calculated by dividing the distance travelled by the substance by the distance travelled by the solvent; R_f values can be used to identify the substance.

sample: a small part of the whole, from which data is collected when it is not possible to count or measure the whole.

serial dilution: the stepwise dilution of a substance in solution.

semi-quantitative test: a test that gives a result that approximates to a value but does not give an exact value (e.g. a glucose concentration of between 0.01% and 0.1%)

Spearman's rank correlation: a statistical test to determine whether two variables are correlated.

stage micrometer: very small, accurately drawn scale of known dimensions, engraved on a microscope slide

stain: a dye that is used to colour specific parts of cells.

standard deviation: a measure of how widely a set of data is spread out on either side of the mean.

standard error: a measure of how likely it is that a mean calculated from a sample represents the true mean for the whole population.

standardised variables: variables that are kept constant in an experiment, which otherwise might affect the dependent variable.

suspension: a mixture of a solid substance and a liquid, where small particles of the solid float in the liquid, but do not dissolve.

systematic error: a source of uncertainty in your results that gives incorrect values that are always of the same magnitude; systematic errors do not affect trends shown by results.

systematic sampling: taking samples at predetermined points.

***t*-test:** a statistical procedure used to determine whether the means of two samples differ significantly.

Practical Workbook Skills

AS Level
AO2 Handling, applying and evaluating information

Legend: ☐ Exercises   ▨ Exam-style questions

Skill	Type	1	2	3	4	5	6	7	8	9	10	11
locate, select, organise and present information from a variety of sources	Exercises		1,4,5,7	1,2	4	1		3	1,2	3,4	1,4	
	Exam-style	6			2,3	3	3		3,5,6	3,4	1,2,3,4,5	4
translate information from one form to another	Exercises	6	1,3,4	2	4	4		4	1,3	3	2,4	
	Exam-style		5	1,2	1,2,3	3		6	1,2,3,6	2,3	1	4
manipulate numerical and other data	Exercises		2,3,4	1,3,5		3			1,2,3	1,2,3,4	2,4	3
	Exam-style	4	2,3,4,5		2			3	2,3	3	5	4
use information to identify patterns, report trends and draw conclusions	Exercises	6	4	2,3	3,4	1	1,3	4	1,2	1,2,3,4	2,4	3
	Exam-style	3	2,3,5,	2	1,2	2,3	1,2	2,3,4,5,6	1,2,3,6	2,3	1,2,3,4,5	4
give reasoned explanations for phenomena, patterns and relationships	Exercises	6	4	1,2	3	4	3	4	1,2,3	2,3	2,4	3,4
	Exam-style	4	2,3,4,5	1	1,3	3	1,2	3,3,4	1,2,3,6	1,2,3	1,2,3,4,5	1,3
make predictions and construct arguments to support hypotheses	Exercises			4							2	
	Exam-style									1		
apply knowledge, including principles, to new situations	Exercises	6		1,3	3,4	1,4	1,3	4	1,2	1,3	2,3,4	3,4
	Exam-style	2,3	1,2,3,6	1,2,3	1,2,3,4	2,3	1,3	2,3,4	1,2,3,5,6	1,2,3,4	1,2,3,4,5	1,3
evaluate information and hypotheses	Exercises											
	Exam-style											
demonstrate an awareness of the limitations of biological theories and models	Exercises								2		4	
	Exam-style							6		4		
solve problems	Exercises		4	2	2			4	2,3	3,4	2,3,4	
	Exam-style		3,5						1,2,3,6	2,3		

AO3 Experimental skills and investigations

Skill	Chapter 1	2	3	4	5	6	7	8	9	10	11
Experimental design											
identify independent and dependent variables		6,	4	2	3		4	4			
choose range, number of values and interval for independent variable, and number of replicates		6,	4	2, 3	3		4	4			
describe an appropriate control experiment						3	4	4		3,4	
use simple or serial dilution		2,3	4	2						3,4	
identify important control variables and how to standardise them		3,6,	3,4 / 3	2	3		4	4		3	
identify methods of measuring dependent variable, including when and how often		6	4 / 1	2 / 1			4	4		4	
assess risk and make decisions about safety			4					2		3,4	
suggest how to modify or extend an investigation to answer a new question			1	3							
Collecting , recording and processing data											
be able to measure an area using a grid								2			
measure using counting, e.g. using tally charts					3			2			
clearly describe qualitative results											
decide how to deal with anomalous results				3				2		4	
measure and record all results to an appropriate number of significant figures											

Skill	_ Chapter _										
	1	2	3	4	5	6	7	8	9	10	11
describe how to identify biological molecules, and use a standardised test to estimate quantity		3, 3,5									
design, construct and complete results charts			4	1, 2, 3	3			1	1,2,3,4		3
show calculations clearly; record calculated values to correct number of significant figures	2, 5,	2,	1	1, 3			4	1,2	1,2,3,4		3
draw graphs; determine the best type of graph or chart to display results		3,	3	1, 2, 3	3		4	1,3	2,		2, 3, 4
calculate percentage change; calculate rate as 1/time and as gradient of line graph			1								
find an unknown value using a graph, including extrapolation		3,	1, 3	3				3 2,3			
describe patterns and trends shown in tables and graphs		2,3	1, 2 2, 3	1, 3 2, 3	4 3		4 6	1,3 1,2,3.6	1,2,3,4 2,3,4	2,4 1,2,3,4,5	4
Evaluating results											
identify significant sources of error, and classify them as systematic or random; calculate percentage error			4	1				2		4	
suggest improvements to reduce error, e.g. by improving standardisation of variables, methods of measurement, quantity of data							4	2		4	
evaluate uncertainty in quantitative results			4					2	4	4	
determine the confidence with which conclusions can be made					4		4	1,2	1,2	2,4	4
make conclusions from data			2,3	1 3	4		4 3,4,	2	1,2 3,4,	2,4 1,2,3,4,5	4

Microscopy and observation of specimens

Skill	Chapter 1	2	3	4	5	6	7	8	9	10	11
use a microscope to identify and draw tissues from prepared slides	3						1,2 / 1,4	1			
calibrate an eyepiece graticule using a stage micrometer, and use it to measure cells and tissues	5										
draw and label plan diagrams							1,2 / 4,	1,			
draw and label details of cells using high power	3						1	4			
use scale bars and magnifications	2,3 / 4			3	1		1 / 4,6	1, / 4			
compare observable features of specimens							1,2,3 / 1,2,4	4	1		

☐ Exercises
▢ Exam-style questions

A Level

AO2 Handling, applying and evaluating information

Skill	Chapter															
	12		**13**		**14**		**15**		**16**		**17**		**18**		**19**	
locate, select, organise and present information from a variety of sources	1,2,4	1,2,3,4	1,4	1,2,3,4	1	1,2,5	1,2	1,2,3,7,8,9	3,4,5,6,7,8	2,3		1,2,3		1,2		1,4
translate information from one form to another	1,3,4	2	1,2,3,4		1,2,4	4,6,7	1,4	1	1,9	4	1,3,4	1,2,3	1,2,3		4	
manipulate numerical and other data	1,2,4		1,2,3	1	1,3,4	3,7	3	1	3		1,3,4	1,2,3	1,2	1,3	4	
use information to identify patterns, report trends and draw conclusions	1,2,3,4	1,2,4,5	1,2,3	1,3,4,5	1,2,3	1,2,3,4,6	1	1,4,5,6	3,4,5,6,7,8	1,3,4	1,3,4	1,2,3,4,5	1,2,3	1,2	1,3,4	
give reasoned explanations for phenomena, patterns and relationships	2,3,4	2,3,4,6	1,2,3	1,3,4,5	1,2,3	1,2,3,4,6	4	1,2,3,4,5,6,7	3,4,5,6,7,8	2,3,4,5		1,2,3		2		2,4
make predictions and construct arguments to support hypotheses			1,3	1				1	3,7			3		2,3		2
information and hypotheses																
apply knowledge, including principles, to new situations	2,3,4	1,2,3,4,5	1,2,3	1,3,4,5	1,2,3	1,2,4,6	1,4	1,2,3,4,5,6	3,4,5,6,7,8	1,2,3,4,5	3,4	1,2,3,4,5	1,2	1,2,3		1,2,3,4
evaluate information and hypotheses																
demonstrate an awareness of the limitations of biological theories and models			2									4				
solve problems	1,2,3,4	1,2,3,4,5	1,2,3	1,3,4,5	1	1,2,6		1,4,5,6	3,4,5,6,7,8	2,3	3,4	1,2,3,5		2,3		1,4

AO3 Experimental skills and investigations

Skill	Chapter							
	12	13	14	15	16	17	18	19
Planning an investigation and describing method								
construct a testable hypothesis		1,3 1	7	1			4	
identify independent and dependent variables	1	1,3 1	1 2,7	1			3 4	
choose range, number of values and interval for independent variable, and number of replicates, and describe how to vary the independent variable		3 1	7	3			4	
describe any appropriate control experiments	1	1,3 1	1 7				4	
make up solutions in %(w/v) or mol dm^{-3} and use serial or proportional dilution		1	2,3	3				
identify key control variables and describe how to standardise them	1,4	1,3 1	1 2,7	1			2 1, 4	
identify methods of measuring dependent variable, including when and how often	1,4	1,3 1	7				4	
describe steps involved in the procedure in a logical sequence		3 1	7				4	
assess risk and describe precautions that would be taken to minimise risk		2					4	
Processing and evaluating data								
decide which calculations are necessary in order to draw conclusions	1,4	1	1,3 7	1	7 2		2 4	
use tables and graphs to identify key points in quantitative data, including variability	1,4 4	1,3 1,4,5	1,4 2,3	1	2	1	2	
draw graphs, including confidence limit error bars	4	1 1	1	1		1 1	2 1	

Skill	Chapter							
	12	13	14	15	16	17	18	19
choose and carry out appropriate calculations to simplify or compare data	1,4	1,3 / 1	4 / 3,7		2,3	1	2 / 44	
use standard deviation or standard error to determine statistical significance of differences between means	1	1 / 1	1			1	1,3	
choose appropriate statistical tests		1,3			7 / 3	1	2 / 4	1
apply statistical methods, including stating a null hypothesis, including t-test, chi-squared test, Pearson's linear correlation and Spearman's rank correlation		3	4 / 7	1	7 / 3		2 / 3	
recognise the different types of variable and different types of data presented	1	1	4	1		1		
identify anomalous results, suggest possible causes and suggest how to deal with them			1					
assess whether replicates were sufficient, and whether range and interval were appropriate		2						
assess whether the method of measuring was appropriate for the dependent variable	4,	1						
assess the extent to which variables have been effectively controlled	4,	1,3						
assess the spread of results by inspection and	1	1						
by using standard deviation and standard error or 95% confidence interval		1						
make conclusions from data	2,4,5 / 2,3,4	1,3	3,4 / 7	6				
discuss how much confidence can be put in any conclusions, including commenting on the validity of the investigation and how much trust can be placed in the data	1,2,4	1,2	3 / 7	6			1,3 / 1 / 1,3	

> Acknowledgements

Thanks to the following for permission to reproduce images:

Cover; Coldimages/Getty Images *Inside* Fig 1.3 Ed Reschke/Getty Images; Fig 1.7 BSIP/Getty Images; Fig 3.5 & Fig 3.6 Geoff and Eleanor Jones; Fig 6.1 & Fig 11.2 Biodisc, VISUALS UNLIMITED /SPL; Fig 6.3 DR KEITH WHEELER/SPL; Figures 6.10, 7.1, 7.3, 7.9, 7.10, 7.11, 7.12, 7.13 BIOPHOTO ASSOCIATES/SPL; Fig 7.2 & Fig 10.3 Alvin Telser/SPL; Fig 7.4 BIOLOGY MEDIA/SPL; Fig 7.6 STEVE GSCHMEISSNER/SPL; Fig 10.2 JOSE CALVO/SPL; Fig 11.1 M. I. Walker/SPL; Fig 11.3 age fotostock/Alamy Stock Photo; Fig 11.5 Dorling Kindersley/ Getty Images; Fig 11.6 GEOFF KIDD/SPL; Fig 12.2 SPL

SPL = SCIENCE PHOTO LIBRARY